THE FAMILY BIBLE COMMENTARY
VOL. V

ADAM C. KOONTZ

---　☩　---

Pauline Epistles, General Epistles & Revelation.

———

AD CRUCEM BOOKS
COLORADO, U.S.A.　:　M.M.XXIV.

Copyright © 2024 Rev. Dr. Adam C. Koontz & Ad Crucem
10394 W. Chatfield Ave., Ste 100
Littleton, CO 80127
United States of America
www.adcrucem.com

Attribution- Non- Commercial- No Derivatives 4.0 International
(CC BY-N C-ND 4.0)

Attribution — You must give appropriate credit, provide a link to the license, and indicate if changes were made. You may do so in any reasonable manner, but not in any way that suggests the licensor endorses you or your use.

Non-Commercial — You may not use the material for commercial purposes.

No Derivatives — If you remix, transform, or build upon the material, you may not distribute the modified material.

No additional restrictions — You may not apply legal terms or technological measures that legally restrict others from doing anything the license permits.

Unless otherwise indicated, all Scripture quotations and references are from the New King James Version®. Copyright © 1982 by Thomas Nelson. Used by permission. All rights reserved.

Unless otherwise indicated, all Book of Concord quotations and references are from the Triglot Concordia: The Symbolical Books of the Evangelical Lutheran Church, 1917, Concordia Publishing House. Public domain.

Jacket and Interior Artwork, Layout Design, and Typographer: Sam Novak.
Layout Artist and Digital Typesetter: Luisa Pasca.
Proofreader: Wanita Wood.
Managing Editor: Timothy Wood.

Typefaces: Adobe Jenson Pro, Montecatini Pro.

Map 1: The Seven Churches of Revelation. Derived from a Bible study published by *The Voice* (The Christian Research Institute).

Map 2, The Roman Empire: Derivative work of "The Maximum Extent of the Roman Empire. Superimposed on a Physical Map" by Andrei Nacu, 2008, Public Domain, Wikimedia Commons.

TO MY CHILDREN

CONTENTS

- Glossary 9
- Introduction 13
- The Epistles of St. Paul the Apostle 17
- Romans 19
  - 1 Corinthians 30
  - 2 Corinthians 40
  - Galatians 48
  - Ephesians 53
  - Philippians 57
  - Colossians 61
  - 1 Thessalonians 64
  - 2 Thessalonians 67
  - 1 Timothy 70
  - 2 Timothy 75
  - Titus 78
  - Philemon 81
  - Hebrews 82
- The General Epistles 93
  - The Letter to James 95
  - The First Letter of Peter 101
  - The Second Letter of Peter 106
  - The First Letter of John 109
  - The Second Letter of John 115
  - The Third Letter of John 118
  - The Letter of Jude 120
- The Revelation of St. John the Divine 125
- Index 145

GLOSSARY

Antichrist – the one who puts himself in the place of Christ (the Greek prefix anti- means "opposite") and thus opposes Christ (2 John 7). He denies the truth of God (1 John 2:2) and may have many allies in his denial, who are thus called "antichrists" (1 John 2:18). He is the "son of perdition" (2 Thessalonians 2:3) whose coming is predicted in the New Testament and fulfilled in the Roman papacy for the reasons laid out in the Smalcald Articles II.IV, especially paragraphs 10-11.

Baptism – the washing of regeneration and renewal by the Holy Spirit (Titus 3:5), which now saves you (1 Peter 3:21).

Bishop – an overseer (1 Timothy 3:1-2, Titus 1:7) of the Christian church, also called an elder (1 Timothy 4:14, 5:17, 19), and in the New Testament, in charge of a local congregation as Titus is to appoint them "in every city" (Titus 1:5). After the time of the New Testament, the term was and still is used for a regional overseer of many congregations.

Church – commonly, a local congregation of Christians (Romans 16:5, 1 Corinthians 6:4, Galatians 1:2, among many); less often, all of God's people in heaven (the martyrs of Revelation 6:10) and on earth (the congregations of Galatians 1:13).

Circumcision – once, the removal of an eight-day-old child's foreskin as a sign of God's covenant with Abraham (Genesis 17:10-14), fulfilled by the Lord Jesus (Luke 2:21), and now supplanted by Holy Baptism (Colossians 2:11).

Conscience – the pain sensed when one has done wrong (Titus 1:15) or the peace sensed when one has done right (2 Corinthians 1:12). It may be wrongly (1 Corinthians 8:12) or rightly (1 Timothy 1:5) informed, but the sense is governed by the information, not the quality of the information. The blood of Christ cleanses it from sin (Hebrews 9:14).

Election of grace (Romans 11:5) – God's choice of His people because of His goodness and Christ's merit apart from anything they are or may be (1 Thessalonians 1:4) so that salvation from before the foundation of the world (Matthew 25:34, Ephesians 1:4) may be all of Him Who calls and not of us (Romans 9:11), lest any man should boast. Also called "predestination" (see Romans 8:29 and Ephesians 1:5).

Fellowship – that sharing with Christ (1 Corinthians 1:9) and with His people (1 John 1:3, 7) in all things (Philippians 3:10) that a Christian may not have with demons (1 Corinthians 10:20, 2 Corinthians 6:14) or with unbelievers (2 Corinthians 6:14).

Gentile – at first and most often, someone who is not a Jew (Romans 9:24), a stranger to the true God (Ephesians 4:18); then, someone who is not a Christian (1 Peter 2:12) because the church is God's people.

Grace – a free gift, especially the free gift of God's righteousness through faith in Christ Jesus (Galatians 2:21), and the opposite of a work (Romans 11:6).

Israel – at first and often, the descendants of Jacob also called "Israel," (Romans 10:1), the people commonly known as the Jews, Paul's own ethnic group (Romans 11:1); especially in the New Testament letters and Apocalypse, the people of God of whatever ethnicity. Thus, the church is the "Israel of God" (Galatians 6:16) or simply "Israel" (Romans 11:26).

Judaism – Paul's former way of life before his conversion to Christ (Galatians 1:13), a pharisaic hostility to the Lord Jesus and to His people (Galatians 1:14) that cannot save a man (Galatians 1:15-16).

Justification – an acquittal and the opposite of condemnation (Romans 5:16); the only justification that avails at God's judgment is for the sake of faith in Christ's work (Romans 4:25, 5:18).

Law – either the natural code known to all mankind (Romans 2:15) or the revealed code given to Moses (Romans 2:23) that convicts men of sin (Galatians 3:19) and shows them how to walk in Christ's way (Romans 8:7, 13:10, 1 Corinthians 9:21, Galatians 5:14); less often and only in Paul, the way that something operates, such as faith (Romans 3:27) or a mind (Romans 7:23); once only, a court of law (1 Corinthians 6:6-7).

Lord's Supper – the meal of His Body and His Blood Jesus instituted (1 Corinthians 11:23)

Nature – God's design for His creation, such as a human body (Romans 1:26, James 5:17), hair (1 Corinthians 11:14), or its dependency on Him (Galatians 4:8); also, the way of something, such as fallen mankind (Ephesians 2:3).

Righteousness – either God's (Romans 3:26) or man's (2 Peter 2:21) capacity to do what is right, especially to deliver on promises made (Romans 1:17). In Christ our righteousness comes altogether from Him through faith (Romans 3:22, Hebrews 11:7).

Sabbath – the seventh day of the week on which God rested from His work of creation and commanded man likewise to rest (Hebrews 4:4), making it a type of the eternal rest found in Christ at the end of our pilgrimage (Hebrews 4:9-11); it need not be a day of rest for Christians (Colossians 2:16), who worship in any case on Sunday, the day of resurrection, the Lord's Day (Revelation 1:10).

Saint – one made holy by God (Philippians 4:21) and, therefore and most often, God's entire church (Romans 1:7).

Satan – the accuser of mankind (Revelation 12:10), a fallen angel also known as the devil (Revelation 12:9) who intends man's destruction (2 Corinthians 2:11) and is the promoter of the Antichrist (2 Thessalonians 2:9).

Sin – a hatred of God and of His law (1 John 3:4) expressed in impiety toward Him (Romans 1:18) and unrighteousness toward one's fellow man (1 John 5:17); the condition of all descended from the first Adam until the last Adam rescues them (Romans 5:16) from its idolatry to serve only Him (Galatians 1:4).

Temple – once, the place of God's dwelling in Jerusalem, a mere copy of the heavenly place of God's dwelling (Hebrews 8:5); now and forever, God's holy people in whose midst He is pleased to dwell (1 Corinthians 3:16, Ephesians 2:21).

Tradition – usually positively, something handed down from one generation or person to the next, such as Paul's supporting himself with his work rather than asking others to support him (2 Thessalonians 2:15, 3:6) or the customs provided to the Corinthians for worship of women's dress and the Lord's Supper (1 Corinthians 11:2); negatively, anti-Christian customs inherited from one's forebears (Galatians 1:14).

Wisdom – the knowledge of God's will (Colossians 1:9) and of how to carry it out (Colossians 4:5), especially in afflictions and trials (James 1:5, 3:17); when it is an evil knowledge of how to carry out sin, the adjectives attached to it clearly distinguish its evil, such as "earthly, sensual, demonic" (James 3:15).

Wrath – God's just punishment of ungodliness (Ephesians 5:6) and unrighteousness (Romans 1:18, 2:5); by extension, man's punishment, either just (Romans 13:4) or unjust (2 Corinthians 12:20), of real or supposed wrongdoing. Christ saves us from God's wrath (1 Thessalonians 1:10, 5:9).

INTRODUCTION

From Christ's fullness, we have all received grace upon grace. His apostles were given the words and boldness to speak them just as He had promised them. Not all received those words as the Word of God, but to those who did receive the apostles' preaching, He has given them the power to become the children of God, born from above water and the Spirit.

These letters and this Apocalypse are that preaching, the very words that Christ gave to His chosen ones and to their disciples such as James and Jude to guide and guard the earliest churches. If men were not sinners and the world were not evil, it is possible these letters would not exist – fourteen of Paul and fourteen of the other disciples of the Lord, counting the seven letters in Revelation. These balanced twenty-eight letters would not have been needful if men listened intently to the preaching of the apostles and guarded it in their hearts.

The letters were written to preserve and extend new churches. They are the letters of missionaries and preachers, not of academicians or bureaucrats. They have the vigor and clarity that the rough-and-tumble of the church's life demands. They show a Christian church scattered already throughout the known world and troubled everywhere by heresies, jealousies, and sheer confusion. People fall away under the pressures of persecution and distraction, and some ministers preach false doctrine shamelessly. This church is very recognizable to us because we see and know it ourselves in our own day. Nothing has changed from that day to this.

That's why these letters were given by the Holy Spirit to them then and to us now afresh. They are not mere historical records of distant times. There are uncertainties about when each of them was written, and our best guess has been provided in the commentary where possible. There are uncertainties about how they were received or to whom some of them were sent, such as in Jude's letter. It is very certain that through them, the Spirit of God is still speaking to His church.

What does He say? Each letter has its own delights, but all the letters of the New Testament affirm that the Old Testament Scriptures pointed to the person and work of Christ Jesus, that Christ came into the world to save all mankind through His death and resurrection, and that when someone believes this, he turns from fruitless service of idols to the fruitful and delightful service of the only true and living God. To these basics, each letter returns us in its way, and from these basics, we are trained to discern good from evil and grow up in the image of Him Who has called us from the darkness of idols into His marvelous light.

What will you find here? The letter's origin, purpose, connections to other parts of Scripture, and its simple literal meaning are laid out for each New Testament epistle and the Revelation to St. John. This is the pure, clear fountain of Israel bubbling over from the fullness of Christ into the life of His holy people in whom His Spirit is dwelling and working. In these letters, it is wondrous to see that the kingdom of God is growing and deepening in the churches despite every external and internal obstacle. The gates of hell did not then prevail against the church of Christ, and through the wisdom and light these letters bring us with all of Holy Scripture, we will be more than conquerors through Him Who loved us.

The Epistles of St. Paul the Apostle

ROMANS

AUTHOR

The undisputed author is Paul the apostle (Romans 1:1), a missionary of the first century AD commissioned to proclaim Christ's gospel to the Gentiles. Since he had already preached as far afield as Illyria (modern-day Croatia), he sought new fields for preaching far to the west in Spain (Romans 15:24, 28). The man who copied down the letter at Paul's dictation, the scribe Tertius, is mentioned, but Paul is the author of the letter.

COMPOSITION AND PURPOSE

Paul writes in the mid 50s AD from Corinth (Phoebe, whom he commends in 16:1-2 lived at Corinth's port of Cenchreae) to Rome because he plans to travel through Rome to evangelize Spain. The letter introduces his teachings ("my gospel," Romans 2:16 and 16:25) to the hearers who first heard it and enlists them to help the gospel's progress around the Mediterranean Sea.

OUTLINE

1:1-17	Introduction and theme
1:18-3:20	Man condemned by the law
3:21-5:21	Man justified only by faith
6:1-8:39	Life in Christ and the struggle with sin
9:1-11:36	The Israel of God and the election of grace
12:1-15:13	Exhortation to life in the Spirit
15:14-16:27	Vindication of the Scriptures and conclusion

CONNECTIONS TO THE OLD AND NEW TESTAMENTS

In the Reformation Romans was used to introduce the entire teaching of the Bible. It was the scaffolding of understanding all biblical theology for Philip Melanchthon in his Loci Communes, the first Lutheran dogmatic theology. Its connections to the Old Testament are numerous since it takes up the meaning of the promises made to the patriarchs and the meaning of the prophets' prediction of the Gentiles' coming to faith. It centers on the theme verse Paul uses here and in Galatians from the minor prophet Habakkuk that the "righteous shall live by faith" (Habakkuk 2:4).

In Romans, one can find almost anything that Paul discusses elsewhere, either at greater length as in the long teaching on how the strong should behave in 1 Corinthians 8:1-11:1 (compare Romans 14) or as in the briefer discussion of justification by faith in Galatians 2-3 that has a much fuller display in Romans 1:18-5:1. Romans is a compendium of Paul's theology and a handbook of the Bible's theology.

Chapter 1

Unknown to the Roman Christians, Paul writes to them and longs to come to see them because the apostleship he has been given is for the "obedience of faith" among all the peoples of the earth. Some of his teaching may be known to them, but he is unknown in person. He thus introduces himself not through human characteristics but by what God has made him to be and the mission God has given him: that the gospel that is the power of salvation should be preached all over the earth.[1]

That gospel is the news about what is wrong with mankind and what God's righteousness has done to set His creation right again. The apostle first goes into what is wrong with men, whose evils extend upward and outward.[2] Upward, men live in impiety or "ungodliness," the lack of fear, love, and trust in the only true God into which sinners are born. The gospel must save such utterly ungodly men.

That ungodliness is always accompanied by "unrighteousness," the hatred of one's fellow man that is expressed in the list the apostle provides in vv. 29-31, extending from outwardly disgusting acts to inwardly defiling thoughts and passions. Such ungodliness and unrighteousness are truly "against nature" because we were not made to be this way. Sin has made us to be this way, with the most terrible example of such unnatural living being when men and women refuse to live together as husband and wife and instead do whatever they want with their bodies, against God's commandment and in a way that harms them. Ungodliness and unrighteousness are unnatural and their own terrible recompense.

From such evils the gospel Paul proclaims must be sufficiently mighty to save. All depends on whether God can or will save such sinners, who may not themselves do all that Paul describes but certainly approve of those who do go to such lengths. Since the evils are so great and so many, everything depends on whether God acts to rescue sinners. That's why "the righteous shall live by faith," Paul's watchword drawn from Habakkuk 2:4. The one who is righteous will find the salvation he needs only in the Lord Who alone can deliver the ungodly and the unrighteous from their plight.

---

1 1·16 is used copiously. At AC XXVIII·9 it is the means whereby eternal things, as eternal righteousness, the Holy Ghost, and eternal life come to mankind. At Ap. IV·67 God cannot be dealt with except through His Word so justification must come through His Word. At Ap. XIII·11 the ministry of the Word has wonderful power. At LC Pref 11 Luther mentions it as the power of God that gives the devil burning pain and strengthens, comforts, and helps us beyond measure. FC Ep. II·4 the preaching and hearing are the Holy Ghost's means of effecting conversion. FC SD V·22 uses it among others to contrast the Law with the Gospel. FC SD XI·29 mentions the Word of God as the means of salvation.
2 1·18 is an encapsulation of the office of the Law (SA III.III.1), alluded to (FC Ep V·8) as what happens when the Law is preached, and Christ explains the Law spiritually to show God's wrath and the greatness of sin (FC SD V·10).

Chapter 2

There could be people among Paul's hearers at this letter's first reading who prided themselves on their descent from Abraham, a Jewishness that would save them by virtue of their birth. Such people pop up in many places in the New Testament, contradicting even the Lord Himself when He shows the uselessness of genealogy in the face of sin's ravages. Paul here pulls back the covering of pride to show how sin is committed secretly even by those who openly condemn it. Some people do some good sometimes, but no man does good all the time. If someone could do good all the time, he would be able to live. The sentence of death and the accusation of guilt would have no power over him, but we are all "without excuse" because whether openly or secretly, our evils are known to God.

All men have God's law written in some measure on their hearts, and some men know the righteous law of God more clearly from knowing the Holy Scriptures. That knowledge does us very little good, even if we should be teachers of that law because it makes it more evident that we are evil. It even causes God's name to be despised because His people do not follow the law He has laid down for their good, our good, and the whole world's good.

What really counts, then, is not what men see or what people imagine might be good or pleasant. What matters is whether someone heeds God's Word. Such a person would not be worried about outward marks of being godly, such as circumcision, but would instead be concerned about his heart being circumcised, whether he has God's Spirit, whether God will praise him for godliness, not what people think is valuable. Men's judgments do not matter at all. God's judgment is everything.

Chapter 3

Is there any advantage to knowing God's law since it only reveals our guilt more clearly or in belonging to God's ancient people, the Jews? Yes, as Paul will later explain, there is a great advantage, but that advantage has nothing to do with God's judgment. He does not show favoritism to one group over another or one person over another. Instead, He reveals His truth to all people in His "oracles" that show forth His will. The unbelief, even of His ancient people, does not nullify His truth. Men's evil and sin cannot overturn His truth and will. Every human being could be revealed as a liar, which would not change the fact of God's truthfulness and faithfulness.

This is the foundation stone of everything else.[3] God's keystone is His truthfulness, so although we need justification because we are ungodly and will have to find justification somewhere other than from our own sinful lives, He needs no justification. His words will always prove true, both in His condemnation of sin and in His provision of a Savior from sin, the Christ Whom Paul proclaims to the nations. The truth is that all men are sinners, as Paul's long chain of quotes from various parts of the Old Testament reveals, but God is the

---

3   The centrality of this chapter and the next in Romans are recognized in the foundational confession, the Augsburg Confession, which cites Romans 3 and 4 as proof in their entirety of the Reformation doctrine of justification by faith (AC IV).

Rescuer from sin and the Savior from death. He puts forth His law so that our mouths can stop talking to justify ourselves and rather quietly listen to His gospel.

That gospel of loving righteousness toward sinners is a gospel of the punishment of One for the forgiveness of all the rest. Paul's words refer to some part or another of the blood sacrifice ceremonies and atonement for sin from the law of Moses. Forgiveness is not free. Someone has to pay for sin. Jesus' blood, more precious than silver or gold, is the currency of salvation. His blood propitiates God and puts away His righteous wrath. Through the shedding of that blood, God is just because He justly punishes all sins in punishing His Son and is the Justifier of the one who has faith in Jesus rather than himself. Justification by faith in Christ rests on Christ's atonement for sin on the cross. Without the cross and the blood and the atonement, there is no justification, and God is not just. His justice and His mercy are both found in the bloody sacrifice of Christ.[4]

Therefore, no one needs to boast in himself because no one is saved through his good deeds, openly or secretly, since all are defiled by sin. All must be justified, Jew or Gentile, the world over, through faith in the only One Who died for sinners and justifies the ungodly through faith in our great High Priest, Christ Jesus.

Chapter 4

The Abraham of whom the Jews were so proud to be descended was not himself an excellent example of the kind of law-based justification they sought. He had once not been circumcised, and he had once not even been named "Abraham," yet he had been justified while a Gentile and while still called "Abram." Since justification comes by faith in God's promise of Christ, the justified man lives not by works as if he were owed it but by grace through trust in God's Word. All the prophets agree on this. Moses wrote of Abraham's justification in Gen. 15:6 when he trusted God, and it was reckoned to him, an unrighteous sinner, as righteousness. David sings of this in Ps. 32 when he describes the justification of the ungodly through faith in the God Who promises forgiveness and life.

Justification isn't an isolated doctrine the Lutherans like to mention on Reformation Sunday or certain other seasons and times. It is the heart of the Bible's teaching because it is how God wants to relate to sinful man: graciously, not according to what we deserve, and by faith, not according to what we have done.[5] If our deserving or our doing were the themes of Abraham's story or David's songs, perhaps justification by works would make some sense. If Moses's law revealed something other than the evils of our sins, then justification by works would be reasonable. Since "the law brings wrath" and since Abraham was justified by faith and David was forgiven by grace, the entire Holy Scriptures witness that God is an entirely gracious God for the sake of Christ's blood and deals with us by way of promises and mercies that we can only trust. The Bible was written for our sake to show that righteousness is "imputed" (4:24) to anyone who believes that Jesus died for our offenses against God's law and was raised for our

---

[4] 3·28 is used in many places in the Book of Concord· as the first example of a particula exclusiva (Ap. IV·73), a summary of "the principal matter of all Epistles, yea, of the entire Scriptures" (Ap. IV·87), as proof that faith alone justifies (SA III.II.4), as an example of the exclusive particles that maintain the chief doctrine (FC SD III·7, 12), faith precedes love necessarily (FC SD III·27), and that St. Paul's doctrine is that faith alone justifies (FC SD III·42).

[5] For an example of the centrality of justification biblically and confessionally, 4·5 makes certain that faith alone is the means and instrument whereby we lay hold of Christ (FC Ep III·3). With zeal and earnestness such exclusive particles must be maintained (FC SD III·7), and its statement is equivalent in meaning to Rom. 3·28, 5·19, and 5·18 in that order (FC SD III·10-13).

justification. The whole plan of God proclaimed throughout the Bible centers on that death and that resurrection so that we might be justified solely by faith in that once-dead and now-risen Jesus.

Chapter 5

Justification by faith is the basis of our peace with God.[6] Without sure justification, we have no peace. With justification, we are at peace with the righteous and holy Creator. With that peace, we learn to endure trials and suffering. The process of change and growth Paul describes in 5:2-4 comes from the love of God the Spirit has given us through faith and points to the love of God we will find in Christ's mercy when He comes again. All we are comes from peace with Christ, and all we shall be will find its goal in peace with Christ.

What we look for at the last day is based on what He is and has done for us already. Since He died for the ungodly before we did or said anything good, we shall surely be saved from God's righteous wrath at the Last Day. The Scriptures pattern the future on the past. What God has done and how God has been is what He will do and how He will be. He is reliable, unlike us, and holds Himself to His Word. If we have already been reconciled to God through Christ, we will indeed find life and mercy in the future with God through Christ.

Our future does not depend on our past but on His work. Our past from our father Adam is a past of sin, with death reigning like some evil king. King Death thought he had us completely under his power, and the slavery to his tyranny was more terrible than we could say. Adam forfeited everything and sold all of us into sin. The last Adam, King Jesus, purchased our redemption from slavery through His blood and brought us into the freedom of His kingdom. What one man undid through sin, the second Man renewed through righteousness. Sin and death were our wicked masters. Now, Christ alone is our Master. Everything created on earth depended on the first Adam, who brought death to power. Everything now depends on the second Adam, who brings life to all believers.

> *Adam is the head of our fallen race, and Christ is the head of God's people. Male headship is not an option within only families that one may or may not adopt. It is how God has designed the human race to function, whether that headship is exercised well in the case of Christ or terribly in the case of our forefather Adam. Adam is responsible for Eve even when he obeys her voice instead of God's. Humanly created structures such as constitutions may recognize the fact of male headship or not, but they cannot abolish what God has instituted. Men are on the hook for better or worse wherever there are families (Ephesians 5:23) or governments (Isaiah 3:12) or churches (1 Timothy 3:1) or any human group.*

Chapter 6

Christians then do not live in sin or indulge sin because sin is part of death's kingdom, and we are no longer subjects of King Death. Our King Jesus is righteous, and we live under His good rule. Sin is no longer our friend since we have been delivered from sin and death through Baptism, which is Jesus' citizenship ceremony, making us His subjects and redeeming us

---

6   5:1 is key to the confessional expression of what justification by faith alone does· the entire doctrine of justification sets terrified consciences at rest (AC XX.15-18) and among many other places in the Apology, Melanchthon says beautifully at IV.91, "Being justified by faith, we have peace with God, i.e., we have consciences that are tranquil and joyful before God."

from slavery under King Death. Baptism is God's means of bringing us into His kingdom and sentencing to death the sin that remains in us even after Baptism. Already, we are dead to sin, and one day, we will be entirely free from sin. Already, we live a new, everlasting life in Christ. One day, we will find that all the promises of the new life will come true.[7]

Because we are on our way to that freedom, sin should not be our pretender king now. We are free from its claims on our past and our future, so we are also free from its claims on our present. We should not present ourselves for service to King Death or Prince Sin because we no longer live in that kingdom. Christ has freed us to be His subjects, so we should present ourselves and our whole bodies, all our "members," for service to Christ. Such service to Christ brings good fruit. The rotten fruit of sin, misery, and death grow only in Death's kingdom. Such bad fruit were our wages for the sin we once lived in. The good fruit of life, peace, and joy grow only in Christ's. Such good fruit is God's gift to us now alive in Christ.

Chapter 7

This chapter's two parts are divided into two parts of the Christian's life: life without Christ and life in Christ. In both parts, sin has something to say to us, but without Christ, we have no response to sin. In Christ, we lay claim to His righteousness against all the claims of sin on us. Though sin is powerful in its deceit and remains even in believers, Christ is mightier.

The law's dominion is sin's dominion. The law is not evil (7:7), as Paul makes clear in many places, but its effect on sinners is to magnify sin. When sinners die in Baptism, they die to the law's claim on them. Now, we live in the Spirit, not by the letters of Moses (7:6). Sin uses the law to awaken evil in sinful men, as Paul attests happened also to him. All this is history for the Christian, and the law and God's commandments remain holy, just, and good.

The change from past tense to present tense in v. 14 is the change from Paul's past to Paul's present. The apostle describes himself as still battling against sin in himself. He is not entirely free from its attacks, though he is not under sin. Sin wants to reclaim him so that King Death can again enslave him, and part of Paul himself wants to be reclaimed and enslaved once more (7:18). His sinful flesh would like to return to Egypt like Israel of old, although God has already freed the slaves.

This struggle with sin is not a sign of despair. It's a sign of hope.[8] The unbeliever has no struggle against sin. Only the believer makes war on his own sinful flesh. Paul's struggle is every Christian's struggle, so Paul's hope is every Christian's hope. That hope cannot be in oneself or one's works or fruit however mature or valuable to the Master anyone may be. That hope will rest one's entire life in Christ, Who delivers from the sin that wants to reclaim us, and the pretender Death, who wants to enslave us once more.

Chapter 8

Just as we are now at peace with God and reconciled through Christ, we are not under His condemnation. How can the one who trusts in Christ's blood have any fear of condemnation?

---

7   At 6·23 this is expressly called a "gift," something to which Melanchthon (Ap. III.235) calls attention to prove that the our beginning and our end in Christ are all of His grace. FC SD XI.81 uses the same verse's other half concerning the wages of sin to attest that the sole cause of damnation in anyone is his sin, not God.

8   7·23 is an expression of this struggle for which private absolution and the use of the Keys are mighty tools against our flesh (SA III.VIII.2).

Whatever power sin may have to enslave, Christ's blood is more potent to free us at last. "Law of sin and death" (8:2) is not God's law as in the "law of Moses." We need not fear the evil way of slavery because we live by God's grace differently: Christ's way, the "law of the Spirit of life." Since Paul does not use the word "law" in the same way in every case, we must carefully examine the context to be clear about how he uses it anywhere.

The death of Christ is the ground of our confidence in freedom. Since Christ fulfilled the "righteous requirement" of God's law, we are free to live by His Spirit and not according to the flesh enticed by sin. God's Spirit works a change in our minds so that we set them on the things of God and not, like Peter forbidding Jesus for predicting His cross and death, on the things of men, the things of the flesh. Even death will be rebuked in our very own bodies when Christ's Spirit raises those bodies from the dead. Sin and death truly never have any claim on Christ's people.

The Christian's life – however full of suffering, weakness, and difficulty – is a life of victory because Christ always wins. Through His suffering, He won. Through His shed blood, He won. Through our suffering and even the shedding of our blood for His sake, He wins. The power on which we draw, by which we refuse sin and put it to death in our bodies, is His power. We do not yet see or know that power's fullness because we await more glories. The whole creation is groaning in anticipation – unable to contain itself or hold it in – of the Day when what Christ has given us is shown to everyone in its fullness. All our life in Christ is like a child waiting for Christmas: a beautiful season, bright, glorious, and looking forward to gifts we can only dream of.

If we now lack words for what we suffer or what we dare to hope, the Spirit is gracious enough to pray with us and for us so that God's children are never without requests to their good Father. This is why Paul now brings up predestination, taught here and in Ephesians 1 and under the heading of "the election of grace" later in this letter. Predestination is not a terrifying verdict by a miserable Judge on a terrified world.[9] Predestination is the Father's assurance to His children that He will get them home – through everything, despite anything, whatever comes. He will get them home, or as Jesus says it in John's gospel, "No one will snatch them from My hand." We who are His shall be His from first breath to Last Day, and He shall be all in all.

Chapter 9

Since His Word is true, what of His ancient people, Paul's own people? This question and Paul's anguish over it occupy this chapter and the next two. If Chapters 1-8 form a unit of Paul's doctrine as he wants to make that clear to the Roman Christians, Chapters 9-11 are a group all about the truthfulness of God's Word and the intention of the Lord to save all who hear and believe His Word of grace.

Thus, the biblical problem of the Jews is not that they are Jews. It is that, generally, they do not believe. Paul is an exception, but in his ministry and the early church's mission to all nations, the Jews were of all the nations of the earth most resistant to the gospel of Jesus. Every man's problem in every nation is his sin and the death that sin deserves. Paul wishes that he could go to hell if it should mean the salvation of his own people. Such love for one's own that you would endure hell rather than see them endure it! In the apostle's voice, we hear the Savior's voice, Who

---

9   Indeed, the Christian meditates on predestination through His Word, "which presents to us Christ as the Book of Life, which He opens and reveals to us by the preaching of the holy Gospel, as it is written in Rom. 8.30, 'Whom He predestined, them He also called,'" (FC Ep. XI.11).

endured all the Father's wrath and death itself so that we might have peace with God that passes all understanding.

Paul here uses "Israel" mostly as he does in Galatians 6 to mean "the Church" or "believers," so that when he says that not all Israel are of Israel, he means that not all ethnic Jews are believers or church members. "Children of the flesh" are not "children of God" unless they also repent and believe the gospel promised beforehand in the oracles of God that He committed to the Jews. God's Word and election stand firm and prove true, and men's preferences for older over younger (Esau over Isaac) and preferences must vanish before God's will. What God desires is what will happen, not what men think or want.

To charge God with unrighteousness is true ungodliness. Men should not do it, but they also cannot do it. If God is God in truth, then what He wants is always good and holy. Men have no right to say to God that He should do otherwise than He does. Since God is God, all things and all men must depend on Him and not He on them. Opening men's hearts to believe and hardening their hearts in unbelief is His choice. If it were otherwise and something depended on men, then the gospel would not be the gospel because we would obtain life through our choice and not His grace.

To witness to this truth, Paul calls many Old Testament passages that all confirm that Israel in its fleshly sense would stumble. However, Israel according to the Spirit, God's people, Christ's Church, would trust in His Word and obtain life and sonship by His grace. What was happening in Paul's day and what happens in ours is always foretold in the Holy Scriptures. Nothing happening should surprise us who know the Bible. The Scriptures show forth the will of the Ruler of the world Who foretold that many would stumble at the gospel's preaching, but many would also believe in the gospel for salvation. This is not what men would have predicted or planned but what God is pleased to do.

CHAPTER 10

The apostle does not deal with abstractions, vague ideas, and opinions of men that may or may not be true. Considering his people's neglect of God's Word, he prays for their salvation. Their zeal is a zeal according to the law so that zeal cannot save them. They will stay far from God as long as they seek righteousness through the law. In Christ and His grace, God draws near to mankind so that only through the gospel is God near to us, not far off.[10] He is so close to us that "everyone who calls on the Name of the Lord shall be saved," the watchword of the Acts of the Apostles and a truth for anyone, Jew or Gentile.

What if they do not believe now? Unbelief must be answered with gospel preaching so that the unbeliever becomes a believer in Christ, not guessing or wishing that somehow he might be saved. Faith comes through hearing the Word of God, and the Word of God is clear that Christ is the purpose and end goal of the law (10:4) for every believer. Yet the Scriptures also witness that Israel according to the flesh has always been stubborn, and God has always had those in all sorts of nations who call on His Name and are saved. What Paul sees playing out before his eyes is the truth God's Word has always proclaimed. Israel's disobedience does not surprise him nor the other nations' obedience of faith to Israel's God. God will be found only through faith in His Christ, whether the believer comes from Paul's nation or any other. This is no new teaching because Scripture unfolds its teaching, never inventing something totally new. The Holy Spirit lays out the meaning of His Word, never contradicting Himself at any time.

---

10 There is no conversion without the preaching of God's Word according to 10·17 quoted at FC Ep. II.4.

Chapter 11

Is the disobedience of the Jews cause for Gentile boasting? Has God forgotten all that He did with and for the Jews in times past? By no means! The natural branch broken off has made space for the wild branch grafted into the tree of Jesse's Son, Jesus. God has not gone back on His promises to save Israel. He has instead made space in Israel for many who are not descended from Abraham, many from all nations, and any who call on His mighty Name. His purposes – His election of grace (11:5-6) – keep for Him a remnant from any nation He is pleased to choose, including the Jews. All this must be of grace, not of works, all of it His choosing, His doing, His giving, His glory, so that no man, Jew or Gentile, may boast except in the Lord.[11]

Election is the ground of certainty, never a cause for uncertainty. As the Formula of Concord insists, the elect has obtained God's salvation solely through His gospel. God's choosing and grace will not be thwarted for His chosen. Election is always accompanied by its opposite, hardening, that blindness of which David spoke, the display of men's unbelief made more terribly clear by the enormity of God's grace in Christ. The reality of vessels of honor the Lord has prepared makes even more horrible the reality of vessels of dishonor devoted to wrath.

Paul's ministry to the Gentiles has a role in the salvation of His people. His prayer and hope are that the Gentiles' salvation through faith will provoke His own people to obtain the same salvation through the same faith, not through the law. The distinction between law and gospel is between two proposed ways of salvation: the Jews have sought salvation through the law but must find it just like the Gentiles through the gospel. Paul is confident that all Israel – Jews and Gentiles – will be saved (11:26) through faith, not through the law or genealogy or whatever other grounds for boasting anyone might have. God has consigned all through the law to the display of their sins that He might have mercy on all through the gospel (11:32).

Chapter 12

Since all believers have such a destiny before them, their lives are changed even now. Their bodies have become the living sacrifices of thanksgiving that, in the Old Testament, dead animals and handfuls of grain signified. God is not building another building of stone in Jerusalem; instead, He is calling all nations to faith in Him and life in Him so that His Name might be glorified through the earth, far beyond Jerusalem. His truth honored each moment in the lives of His people, not only at appointed times of day or year as in the temple of old.

That honor is expressed through the church's conformity to Christ, not to the world. That conformity involves virtues that fit into the larger body of Christ (12:3-8). No Christian is given a spiritual gift from the Holy Spirit for showing off. His gifts are for the greater good of the body, which is Christ's, not his. Some gifts vary from one another, aligning with one's role in the church. Still, most gifts and tasks are common to all: avoidance of hypocrisy, abhorrence of evil, patience, steadfastness in love, and hospitality. 12:9-21 are a longer explanation of the fruit of the Spirit than one finds in Galatians 5-6, but the substance is the same. In each list, the church has plenty to consider in each phrase and each sentence so that each Christian finds his unique place in the body through the common practices we all share. In submission to one another out of love, we

---

[11] The chapter's conclusion at 11-33 is cited in the Formula to distinguish clearly between His powers and ours so that our method of understanding Him must be, "…since God has reserved this mystery [of election] for His wisdom…Rom. 11-33ff, we should not reason in our thoughts, draw conclusions, nor inquire curiously into these matters, but should adhere to His revealed Word, to which He points us" (FC SD XI.55).

find freedom. In sacrifice for one another, we find true wealth. In all things, we find conformity to Christ the sort of change in one's image that the years make better, not worse.

CHAPTER 13

The enemies at the end of ch. 12 escape the Christian's private wrath because God has appointed the powers that be – the various levels of government – for the particular purpose of punishing with His public wrath. The express reason for the existence of government is to use the sword, an instrument of destruction and death, to uphold goodness and punish evil. This chapter is not intended to allow governments to do or say anything they like. Their limits are known from Nebuchadnezzar's and Pharaoh's evils and from the limits expressed by the apostles themselves. Instead, Paul clarifies what the purpose of government is and why it bears the power of life and death for this life only. It has no power over eternal life or eternal death because its limited purpose is stopping outbreaks of wickedness and vengeance in this life on this earth.

> *Human governments may take on many tasks, but their basic purpose, according to Romans 13, is the administration of justice – punishment to evil and reward to the good. If that is not accomplished but many tax breaks are given, or pension plans are made solvent, or roads are fixed, then the purpose of the government has not been accomplished. The sword is given to punish the wicked and defend the good, as it was in the beginning of human society after the Flood in Genesis 9. Government keeps the order in daily life that makes tax collection, pensions, and road repairs possible, whoever sees to those things. Without order, there is no sense in government, and anarchy would prevail – a terrible thing in a world full of sinful men.*

That limited purpose informs the Christian's support of the government through his taxes and other revenue payments. He need not do it begrudgingly because he is not an anarchist. He understands that swords and order cost money to maintain. None of it is easy, and the government may indeed overstep its bounds, as it is wont to do in many places and times. In all things, the believer must love his neighbor and fight his flesh because the government knows nothing of his struggles. The government must struggle against open evils of flesh and blood, but the Christian makes war in the heavenly places against Satan, and through Christ, Who loves him, is more than a conqueror. That is an empire, a kingdom, a war, and a victory of which princes and governments know nothing and can do nothing for or against.

CHAPTER 14

This chapter has its direct and extended parallel in 1 Corinthians 8:1-11:1, where a fuller discussion with extended examples is available. Paul is not specific here as he is there because the issue may be a general difficulty rather than a special, particular stumbling block as it was in Corinth. Yet the reason there are some Christians who eat only vegetables in Rome is the same as it was in Corinth: the desperate desire to avoid all meat lest some meat offered in some way at some time to pagan idols be consumed. As in 1 Corinthians, the apostle encourages the strong, who know that idols are nothing and meat was made to be received by God with thanksgiving, not to quibble and quarrel but to be gentle with weak brothers, as Christ is gentle with the weak and tenderhearted.

The pattern Christ gives is not an encouragement to anyone to remain weak. Still, since the strong are in greatest danger of disregarding the other brothers, Paul admonishes them, not the weak, who are by definition in need of improvement in their knowledge of God's will and their walk according to that will. The love that must prevail among both weak and strong is the same love with which Christ loved us and gave Himself up for us, a fragrant sacrifice to God and a blessing to His body. We are not free to do or say whatever we please because we belong to a body that needs our help and the nourishment we can bring. In everything, I live for my brother, not my brother for me, because Christ came not to be served but to serve, so I must do likewise.

Chapter 15-16

As the Scriptures bore witness to Israel's disobedience, they also foretold that Christ would live and die and live again for the salvation of the Gentiles as well as the Jews. Paul's ministry, perhaps controversial among some in Rome, was amply predicted centuries earlier in the Old Testament Scriptures. The Scriptures have always filled all believers with comfort so that their hope should be firm, not wavering. Paul envisions not halfhearted Christians somewhat interested in Christ. For him, all the church, Jew and Gentile, from every nation confidently believes and confesses that Jesus is the Savior of all nations.

Since among the nations Paul had gotten as far as modern-day Croatia (Illyricum), he is bold to push God's promises of salvation for everyone who calls on His Name still further. He would like to stop to see the Romans on his way to preaching in Spain. He must first bring the priestly offering of the Gentiles' contribution for the Jews' good to the impoverished Jewish Christians in Jerusalem. Still, he desires God's protection and the Romans' prayers to find his way farther in the gospel's service.

His unusually extensive list in ch. 16 is because he does not know the Roman churches. He, therefore, hazards nothing in listing everyone he knows because he can scarcely forget anyone, having never before been there. He knows so many because Rome was connected to so much. Truly, all roads at this time did lead to Rome, and many were from Rome. Similarly, today, many of us are from California, Florida, Texas, and New York, the states with the most people. He knows people with Greek names, Jewish names, and Latin names, and as with the rest of his ministry, he is grateful for both men and women assisting his ministry. He does not know the names of people who may be causing division in the body, but such division is sinful to cause, so the Romans should note and then avoid people who cause division, who want to divide Christ in His body.

Like almost all Paul's letters, this one is long enough that others take their opportunity to send greetings. Romans is especially long, so we have the name of Tertius written down because he was the scribe who copied the thing out for Paul. Tertius may have written the last couple of verses on the outside of the letter after it was folded as a blessing to the carriers and the readers who would bear it to Rome. Still, whether found in the original body of the letter or on its cover, the blessing matches the prologue of the letters sixteen chapters earlier: Christ was predicted from long beforehand in the Holy Scriptures, and now His salvation is proclaimed to all nations. The nations now render Him the obedience only faith gives to God's Word.

1 CORINTHIANS

AUTHOR

Paul had written beforehand to the Corinthians (1 Corinthians 5:9) and now write along with his coworker Sosthenes (1:1) to make clear what must occur in this divided, confused congregation.

COMPOSITION AND PURPOSE

Paul had yet to take the collection he had made for the Jerusalem church with him at Pentecost (1 Corinthians 16:8), so this letter was written sometime during his stay in Ephesus (Acts 18:18-19:41), that is, during the years 53-57. This most matter-of-fact of his letters was written to set straight what had become crooked in the Corinthian church he had founded earlier, mainly because he had received reports from congregation members of the church's problems (1 Corinthians 1:11).

OUTLINE

1:1-9	Introduction and thanksgiving
1:10-4:21	Is Christ divided?
5:1-6:20	Worldliness in the members
7:1-40	Marriage and singleness
8:1-11:1	Worldliness and the weaker brother
11:2-34	Apostolic tradition and Corinthian departure from it
12:1-14:40	Spiritual gifts in worship and love in all things
15:1-58	The resurrection goal
16:1-24	Taking leave and the collection for Jerusalem

CONNECTIONS TO THE OLD AND NEW TESTAMENTS

1 Corinthians is indispensable to understanding the practical problems of the Gentile mission and the reason for so much alluded to in 2 Corinthians. Here, we see a congregation struggling to adjust to the boundary between God's holy people and an unholy world, attempting to be neither too lax nor overly harsh.

Less obvious is that 1 Corinthians mostly quotes from the prophet Isaiah in its direct quotations. Though much of the discussion of issues is based on what is going on in Corinth rather than which passages of Scripture Paul would like to discuss, the apostle's overall understanding of wisdom and God's surpassing glory in Christ runs through

Isaiah, especially its first third where the prophet describes how God will vindicate His Name despite men's foolishness.

Chapter 1

This chapter is a marvel of unity in a letter to a divided church. Unity in Christ is its source and theme, unifying all that Paul will say throughout the succeeding fifteen chapters. It is an overture to a symphony in which one hears almost all of the sounds from the top, which will be played at greater length later on.

Unity is found in "Christ and Him crucified" (2:2), and that was and is the heart of Paul's preaching to the Corinthians (1:18). Why? Because the Son of God is the power and wisdom of God, and anything men may desire or seize is foolish in light of His cross. Apart from that crucified Christ, the Corinthian church has no wisdom, goodness, beauty, or anything it may boast of. In that crucified Christ, the Corinthians may boast because they boast in the Lord (1:31).[12]

In all the various things that follow in the letter, remember that Christ crucified is the beating heart of the letter's body. He is the foundation for the whole building of the church (ch. 2-3) and the message and the life of His apostles (ch. 4). His wisdom and resurrection are the reason we must live in fear of God and not walk according to the flesh (ch. 5-7). He will be the pattern of Paul's behavior and the Corinthians' expected behavior (ch. 8-10). His teaching is why the church must not behave like the world (ch. 11) because they have not learned a Christ who conforms to the world. Rather, they must be conformed to Christ (ch. 12), Whose crucifixion is the ultimate demonstration of what love is (ch. 13). Their entire worship must edify His Body with His Word (ch. 14) because He is coming soon to raise His Body from the dead (ch. 15). All things flow from and back to the Cross in this letter of unity.

Chapter 2

The Holy Spirit is not a cloudy idea Paul had and then confused with his own emotions. The Holy Spirit comes to men through the preaching of Jesus' cross, so whether Paul was powerful himself or not (2:3), the Spirit was and is at work among the church through God's power in Jesus' cross. That power is also true wisdom, but those reckoned as wise in any age do not know that sort of cross wisdom because the cross and its purpose of rescue from sin and death seems foolish to them (2:6).

Jesus' resurrection means that this age of folly is ending. All of this is according to God's choice, not man's, because man does not know what he is truly doing nor where he is truly heading unless God shows him and leads him, and teaches him. We do not understand Him or ourselves naturally,[13] but God's Spirit, Who knows and searches all things, must teach us. That is why the one who is "spiritual," who has and is filled with the Holy

---

12 "…we cannot boast of many merits and works, if they are viewed apart from grace and mercy, but as it is written, 1 Cor. 1·31, 'He who boasts, let him boast in the Lord,' namely, that he has a gracious God,'" SA III.XIII.3.

13 Per 2·14, the heart cannot render the true works of the First Table of the law without the Holy Spirit, Ap. XVIII.73.

Spirit, "examines all things" (2:15), and why we "have the mind of Christ" (2:16). God has given us these gifts so that we would be neither worldly as if we did not have God's Spirit nor foolish as if Christ's mind were not ours. The Corinthians tend both to worldliness and to foolishness in many and various ways because they have forgotten who they are in Christ through the Spirit.

Chapter 3

Such forgetting is the source of their divisions. They attach themselves to various pastors they know (3:5) because they have forgotten that Christ is not Himself divided. The church is not unified in anything other than Christ. There is no unity in Paul, Luther, Calvin, this pope, or that bishop. There is only unity in Christ, and all the preachers must be servants of Christ, proclaimers of Christ's wisdom, not their own, because there is genuinely no other possible way to build the church than through Jesus Christ (3:11).

Chapter 4

The preachers, whether someone boasts of them or not, are stewards of God's things, like the priests and Levites in the old temple who did precisely what God told them to do. Paul is unconcerned about human judgments because he is very concerned about divine judgment (4:4). He is accountable – as is any minister of Christ – to Christ for his work and worth, and Christ will soon come to weigh all those things and praise faithful servants (4:5).

The way of a steward is the way of his master. Paul has lived, and lives, as did and does his Master, Jesus, trading his sadness for the joy of those he serves (4:9-13). Sacrifice for the Corinthians is his way because it is Jesus' way with and for all of us.[14] The Corinthians have forgotten this very practical lesson: it is enough for the disciple to be like his Master. You cannot live unlike Christ and yet belong to Christ. If you are in Christ, you live like Christ, giving up oneself for others. Since this is practical, Paul reminds the Corinthians of his personal example, not a mere whiteboard lesson (4:15) such as any tutor might give, and he sends Timothy in the flesh to this congregation to show them how to live in Christ as he does and as disciples must do (4:17).

To the Corinthians, he is no mere preacher but their father, the closest thing to the ongoing relationship in Christ that a pastor has with his congregation one will find in Paul's letters. Like a father, he may chastise or praise them (4:19-21). Consequently, they have a choice in front of them as the apostle launches into the many assorted issues they face: will they conform to Christ as they have learned Him from Paul's ways and words, or will they conform to the world as they have learned its ways from Satan and their own flesh?

Chapter 5

The letter moves from least common and most egregious offenses to more common

---

[14] All ministers of Christ may expect the same. Luther cites 4.13 in the Large Catechism, 4th Commandment, 158-160, to say, "…they must be (as St. Paul says, 1 Cor. 4.13) as the filth of the world and everybody's refuse and footrag."

and less horrifying sins. This chapter concerns the most terrible transgression permitted in Corinth and why the church must discipline itself. A man has taken his stepmother for his wife, something the "Gentiles," not here a racial group but simply all unbelievers, would not even do. Satan likes to display his work in making God's people do more heinous things than the Gentiles do.

The Corinthians must cast the man out of the church – delivering him to Satan the accuser (5:5) – so that his flesh, with its evil desires, may be mortified or destroyed through exclusion from the communion of the saints. The church is a product of Easter, so the leaven that was all right before the feast of deliverance from death is no longer tolerable. It must be cast out of the house. Certain things are intolerable in the church because they affect everything else, and the boasting in which the Corinthians indulge about their congregation (5:6) is absurd since they allow such evils to go on in their midst. For the man's and church's sake, the man must be put out of the church until he repents.

This judgment on a member is not a judgment on the world, which is God's to render. In the church, the realities of the Last Day have already begun: we already know what God loves and what He hates, what to do, and what to leave undone. We cannot neglect such knowledge and pretend that nothing matters and that everyone can live as he sees fit. Such delusions and lies are Satan's. Instead, we must judge ourselves according to God's Word and not permit what God says is evil. The Corinthians are not seeking judgment and discipline in the church. Instead, they want no judgment in the church and seek judgment instead from secular courts.

Chapter 6

In a worldly court, brothers sought judgments against one another. Paul recommends instead that a wise brother hear and judge the dispute among brothers. Why this parallel situation? Are courts evil? No, but it is evil for Christians to pretend that their property or civil complaints matter more than their baptism. It is evil for Christians to defraud or defame their brothers rather than seek peace with one another. How can any court give you what the Lord can provide in forgiveness and mercy? Therefore, stand before the church for judgment before you worry about what the Gentiles may be able to offer you.

A self-seeking way of life belongs to the time before the Corinthians were converted, when they were idolaters, because idolatry always gives plenty of room for the flesh to pursue its satisfaction (6:9-11). The Christian life is different from worldly life because it has its source in the washing of Baptism, the holiness of God's Spirit, and the justification Christ brings (6:11). So, not everything is permissible or good for Christians to do. In contrast, some things belong to idolatry, others to the Spirit of God. Some in Corinth claimed they could do what they wanted with their bodies against the Sixth Commandment (6:16) because they were the Lord's. But the Lord's claim is a claim not only of love but also of possession. He is merciful and jealous, and what is His must always be His. What He bought at the price of His own blood, He does not lightly give up (6:20).

Chapter 7

As the Body is Christ's, one's body must serve Christ's purposes, in or out of marriage. It seems that some in Corinth thought marriage should be avoided entirely, but Paul disagrees with that for most people and provides several guides to keeping the marriage bed undefiled.[15] If one chooses not to marry, he is free, as is Paul, to pursue whatever purposes God has for him, but if he does marry, he must live for the other as Christ lives for His Church, His Body.

Marriage is a remedy for sin. Whether one is considering marriage (7:2) or one is already married but not living as closely together in marriage as you might (7:5-6), married life is an antidote to the venom of sin. If one chooses to remain unmarried, one will also not be distracted as married people often are with earthly concerns (7:33), but a little distraction is better than burning without self-control (7:5).

Once one has been married, several things are clear. Marriage lasts until death, and only at death is a person free from the marriage partner (7:39). The exception to that bond is when that bond has been broken and cannot be repaired because the husband or wife has disappeared and does not return (7:15, to which you can compare the other exception in Matt. 19:9). If a Christian's spouse is an unbeliever, that is not grounds for divorce (7:13), but that is true only when you were converted to Christ after having been married. If you are unmarried, you should not marry an unbeliever. You must marry a Christian (7:39). These teachings on marriage are not merely "traditional"; indeed, some of them, such as the wife's right over her husband's body in marriage (7:4), were not at all "traditional" in the first century. These teachings are spiritual and aimed at preparing Christians, whether they marry or remain unmarried, for the coming of Jesus (7:29) when all must account for what they have done in the body. Therefore, flee sin in the body, since it is so grievous to the soul and the body, and pursue a godly life.

Chapter 8

The godly use of one's time and life is the crux of the matter in Corinth, where many claim to know much of the Lord (8:1) yet live contrary to His teachings. They especially love to go ahead with their own inclinations and disregard their brothers, who have different convictions about the line that distinguishes worldliness from godliness. This has come to a head in Corinth around the meat sacrificed to pagan idols and distributed in ancient cities through pagan temples. Some in Corinth eat it freely. Some refuse ever to eat any meat lest they eat such sacrificed things. Where does the line lie between what is acceptable for Christians and what is not?

Paul answers that question through the Body. He does not consider one's behavior apart from the Body. In this long answer occupying the lion's share of three chapters, he begins with several truths about idols and the meat sacrificed to them. The idols are indeed nothing, as many Corinthian Christians claim (8:6), and the meat sacrificed to

---

15 The confessional argument for a married clergy is based on 7.2, 9, especially that forbidding marriage is against nature, AC XXIII.4.

them was created by God like all other food to be received with thanksgiving. Yet, the Body does not all have the same strength. Some parts are weak precisely because they have been formerly idolatrous (compare 8:7 to 6:9-11).

Previous acquaintance with some sin makes a person sensitive about that sin, particularly when another Christian cannot or does not agree that it is a sin in any way. How can food matter to a Christian? Jesus, in Mark 7, declared all foods clean. Idols are nothing, and food is an indifferent matter (an adiaphoron in theological terms). Why, then, can I not eat whatever I want? I cannot do whatever I want whenever I want because some things are sinful, and some things are not, which may prove harmful to my brother, who does not know the difference. "Weak" in this chapter means a conscience that is too sensitive (8:12). My brother should stop being weak, but before I demand that he stop, I will first do whatever I can to help him and help his salvation rather than have him fall once more in his weakness (8:13).

Chapter 9

The governing principle of doing what is for the brother's good is seen and known in Christ's cross and Paul's walk in Christ's ways. The apostle's first-person speech about what he is free to do and what he does, and the difference between the two is a speech about sacrifice. He is free to take a wife (9:5) as any minister is and as most other apostles have done. He is free to be paid by the people who hear him preach the gospel (9:6-14), whether he draws a salary from them or not. "Free" could be thought of here as "license" or even "right" rather than a negative freedom not to do something. Paul has a claim on a wife in the Lord if he so chooses and on support from those who hear the gospel, but he lays aside that license or those rights to not burden a wife with his constant travel or a new congregation with the responsibility to pay him.

Paul's conduct is governed by the cross, not by his rights. The cross is a forsaking of one's license or rights for the brother's benefit. He offers the gospel "free of charge" (9:18) because it enables it to be preached even to those who cannot support a minister. Sacrifice is freedom. He sacrifices his freedom from the law of Moses to live under it for the sake of the Jew (9:20). He sacrifices his freedom to be a Jew for the sake of the Gentile who does not live under such a law (9:21). Such sacrifice is the "law of Christ" that he is under and that he elsewhere defines as bearing one another's burdens (Gal. 6:2), whether of being Jewish or being Gentile or being weak. Jews, Gentiles, and weak Christians may all eat very different food according to very different laws. The strong Christian is free not to obey their manmade laws and free to obey such laws so that he may evangelize the Jew, the Gentile, or the weak brother. All he does is for the sake of the other, not for himself. Living for oneself is a way of indulgence that Paul fears even for himself lest he fall into it (9:26-27).[16] The way of discipline and self-denial is the way of life for Paul because it is Christ's way (9:24), the way of victory in the end.

---

16 Such discipline of the body helps to fulfill one's callings, AC XXVIII.37-39, because the Old Adam in a believer must be driven not only by the Law but also by punishments, FC SD VI.19, both citing 9:27.

Chapter 10

The Corinthians are not unusual, nor is Paul unusual in facing such dangers along the way. "Our fathers," whether we are Jews or Gentiles, are the Old Testament Christians, God's Israel, who faced the same dangers and temptations we do. Yet many saw God's wonders and nonetheless fell in the wilderness, walking by God's wrath (10:5, 10). These Scriptures are "examples" (10:6, 11) to us so that we do not do the same thing they did. When we see their fall, as when the Corinthians would have witnessed the excommunication of the adulterous man in chapter 5, the purpose of the church is for each to look to his own sin, his own flesh's inclinations, and know that he is not the first to deal with such problems nor is God leaving him to his own devices. All idolatry must be fled. Everyone has a merciful God willing and ready to provide a way out of the wilderness at the last (10:13).

Flight from idolatry, which is flight from any sin, is imperative for all Christians, and Paul draws out that logic of what to do about meat sacrificed to idols in pagan temples from the facts of the Lord's Supper. Paul is asking rhetorical questions because no one in Corinth doubts that the bread is Christ's Body and the wine is Christ's Blood (10:16). His questions lead to thinking about how sharing in the Lord's table affects the rest of one's life. If you share with Christ, how can you share with demons? It is the same problem of mixing or adulteration (from which we get the word "adultery" in the Sixth Commandment) that the Corinthians have in their use of worldly courts detailed in chapter 6 and the confusion about marriage discussed in chapter 7. They do not know what being the Body means.

Can the Body live in communion with demons? No, not at all because the Lord is jealous and mighty (10:22). He cannot stand to share His Body with another Bridegroom (Eph. 5:23). She is His. Thus far, any Corinthian Christian would agree, so Paul makes clear what kind of behavior they should engage in so that the weak brother may not stumble (8:13). If one gets some meat and no one says that it's been dedicated to an idol, well and good. Anything may be eaten with thanksgiving to the Creator (10:25). Even a meal with an unbeliever at his home is well and good. Still, if that unbeliever tells you how it has been devoted to an idol, you should not eat, lest his conscience be informed that the true God and the false gods are somehow the same. The issue with eating meat is never about the meat itself. Christianity has no specific food laws like almost every other religion. Christianity has a particular attachment to Jesus' way of life in service to the conscience of all mankind, so if someone's conscience is confused by your actions, do not take that action. Ensure that the weak brother and the unbeliever understand that there is salvation only in the Name of the true God. On my own I may eat anything. For the sake of another and for the salvation of mankind, I will do whatever I can in the law of Christ. That way Paul commands the church to imitate because it is his way and Christ's way (11:1).

Chapter 11

The two traditions Paul had given the Corinthians were both concerned with divine worship. In worship, the women covered their heads, and the Lord's Supper was given out according to the Words of Institution he had recited for them. Since they are puffed up with a certain kind of knowledge, the Corinthians have departed from these apostolic traditions and begun to conduct worship in their own manner, with women and men looking very similar and the Lord's Supper largely discarded in favor of a potluck feast.

The covering given to women is either a veil or other hat or their natural hair. The Corinthians reversed a natural order by having men with heads covered as if they were under authority and women with heads uncovered as if they were not under any authority.[17] This reversal is an inversion of their divinely created sexes. The symbol or covering the woman wears will put things right-side-up. Their hair is itself a covering (11:15), and the created orders God established should be expressed in one's daily life. Wearing a covering "because of the angels" (11:10) means that the woman's life and dress conform to the divine order the angels themselves maintain (Psalm 103:20). Corinthian foolishness must submit to divine wisdom.

In the Lord's Supper, they are still more remiss, and the apostle's tone changes between the chapter's two sections from correction to incredulity. His incredulity proceeds in three steps: description of their foolishness, reminder of Christ's own practice, and push to examine themselves. The drive to examine oneself (11:28) is not then a justification for denying communion to children until a particular age. It is a demand for reflection and repentance on a group of adult Christians who have altered the Lord's Supper into an occasion for getting drunk (11:21), forgetting that the Supper is Christ's Body and Blood and that the church is the Body of Christ. Their thoughtlessness has caused many to partake of the Lord's Supper without discernment and pushed them headlong into sickness and even death (11:30) because they refuse to see the Lord's judgment at work in the church even now as it will be at the Last Day (11:31). The Corinthians live even in the church's worship as if the Last Day shall not come. Already, their heedless transgressions catch up with them. They must change their practices in worship because in worship, they are meeting and treating with the Lord, not with one another merely, where they could eat and drink how and what they like and dress how they want. Since worship is when and where the Lord is with His Church before that Day, judgment begins already with the household of God (1 Peter 4:17).

Chapter 12

The presence of God's Spirit in the church is unity's cause, not division's origin. Yet few things have caused more division in the church's history than this or that person or group's claims to possess the Spirit in special measure. The Spirit is given to each for all. At that time, the Spirit of God gave gifts of languages to communicate with new people-

---

17 AC XXVIII.53-54 understands the Pauline admonition for women to cover their heads as a manmade ordinance useful for order in the church.

groups, as He had at Pentecost, as well as gifts of administration and preaching (called "prophesying" here) and many other gifts. There is no particular distinction between the office of the ministry or any other work in the church in this chapter because the issue is not an issue between clergy and laity but among a body that does not think of itself as a body.

> Unsurprisingly, the Corinthians had so many difficulties in worship, as discussed in chapters 11, 12, and 14 of this letter. In worship, man's nearness to God heightens either his rebellion as in the worship of the golden calf (Exodus 32) or his submission to God in the worship of the returned exiles (Nehemiah 8:6, 9:3). In worship we find out who we really are and what we really believe as the old church adage has it, lex orandi, lex credendi, that is, the law of praying is the law of believing. How we pray – whether disordered as in Corinth or otherwise –determines what we believe and demonstrates what we believe.

Instead, the Corinthians think of these gifts as individual attributes. The apostle is clear that the gifts are for the benefit of the body (1:7). Division is rife whenever people envy one another's gifts rather than developing their own. This envy, sometimes called "equality" by modern people, is why Paul asks rhetorically whether everyone has a particular gift (11:28-30) because many want to be everything in the church and cannot stand to be what God has given them. Their lack will become evident in the next chapter when they fail to have that gift that should be common to all in the Body of Christ: love that holds all together.

Chapter 13

The Christian without love is like a musical instrument useful in divine worship but unable to fathom what it means. The cymbal clangs and has no sense of eternal judgment. The brass rings and cannot know that the Lord is in the midst of His people. Love for and in the Body is the mark of Jesus' friends and endures when all other gifts and instruments fall aside (13:10).

Love describes the Lord Himself, and so describes His Body. Vv. 4-7 describe any time in the Lord's ministry, life, death, or resurrection, and they represent His people who live in His one Body. Love is the life of Christ already resurrected in the flesh on the third day and already begun in His holy Temple, His Body, the Church, through the Spirit given to us. Like all else about Paul's call to imitate Christ (11:1), the call to love has its pattern in Christ's patient, hopeful, kind sacrifice for mankind. The Corinthians have not been living according to that pattern, and their lovelessness had unraveled their life together.

A Christian who is loveless is not emotionally stunted or whatever psychological term one might use. A Christian who is loveless does not see that the Lord is alive and living amid His people now and shall come on the Last Day. He has missed the presence of the Lord as surely as the Corinthians did not understand that the angels looked on at their worship and that the Lord's Body and Blood were there in ch. 11. A Christian who is loveless misses everything, and when the world matures into its fullness, and Jesus comes again, all faith and hope and good works and gifts fade, and only love abides (13:13). Invest in what lasts, most of all.

Chapter 14

Boasting and confusion – so characteristic of Corinthian marriage problems and internal divisions – are found clearly in their worship services. English Bibles use the word "tongues" most commonly for what we know as "languages" in ordinary speech. Some at Corinth have been given the gift of speaking in other languages as the apostles had at Pentecost because Corinth was large enough and wealthy enough to have people from many nations. It would be an excellent advantage for spreading the gospel to learn to speak other languages very quickly.

Yet, such languages required interpretation for the majority who would have spoken Greek. Like the other gifts they possessed, they neglected to think of one another, using God's gifts, preaching in foreign languages, and doing whatever they pleased. This is accompanied in their congregation by an insistent bringing forth whatever gift one may have had for display, and general confusion ensued in their worship. No one was edified because confusion reigned.

Paul calls them back to order not out of some personal fussiness but because God is a God of order (14:33). He does not author the confusion of the sexes (14:34) or of languages (14:31) the Corinthians demonstrate. Notice that their lovelessness is accompanied by their confusion when together. People without love do not know what to do with others when they are present, and none know how to conduct themselves in the house of God where the Lord Himself is present. They have misunderstood His gifts since He gave languages as a sign for unbelievers and prophesying or preaching (in the common language of the place) for believers. Unforeseen speaking of a language the speaker had yet to learn signals to the unbeliever that something mighty and wondrous is afoot. The believer is built up through the regular preaching of God's Word in a language he understands. The Corinthians, in their confusion and boasting, are putting neither the gift of languages nor of preaching to good use. They might right their course.

Chapter 15

Here, the apostle sings of victory, love, and the death of death. He must sing because without rising to these heights with him, the Corinthians cannot see the purpose of the changes they must make or the prize to which they must press forward together. They will remain mired in their divisions and petty fiefdoms without understanding how Christ's resurrection changes their daily lives now.

As with all else in Corinth, some have grasped this truth and yet perverted it in practice because they were being baptized on behalf of the dead (15:29), trying to bring even those already having faced judgment (Hebrews 9:27) into Christ's Body through Baptism. After death, it is too late for repentance and baptism. Now in this life is the time for change, and the Corinthians must radically change their life in Christ so that they can undergo the radical change Christ has for them in the resurrection. The extended comparisons of different sorts of glory and bodies in the Lord's creation are the ground as in a parable of Jesus for the realities of the kingdom of heaven. What we will be is now what we now are because the Last Day will bring in a new season for the universe as cold winds bring rain and snow at the year's end.

The moral commands of this chapter are general because Paul has no specific problem in mind, unlike in the previous chapters. If the Corinthians cannot grasp the scope of the change in the universe that Christ's Last Day will bring, they can grasp nothing. He must give large warnings such as "do not sin" (15:34) because significant things such as the changing of resurrected man into the image of the Resurrected Man and the abolition of death are in view. Here, he sings as he did in chapter 13 when eternal love was in view because that is what the saints do in the resurrection: they sing to and of the Lamb.

Chapter 16

Paul's plans for the winter and reminders of various coworkers in the gospel to and for the Corinthians seem a poor fit for the heights and depths of chapter 15. What does a man's itinerary have to do with the resurrection of Jesus? Everything in the world since that man carries the life of Jesus with him in the message he preaches and the life he lives. By no accident is the final practical matter of the letter about Paul's collection for the churches in Judea who had suffered much at the hands of their fellow countrymen, the Jews.

The instructions for giving to the collection bring the Corinthians into a fellowship of self-sacrifice to which Paul belongs, a communion with Christ in living for others and not for oneself. Paul is asking the Corinthians to be Christians in Christ's way and to care for the Body through their gifts laid aside on the Lord's Day. The churches in Judea may have been skeptical of Paul (Acts 15) and his ministry. They may not have contributed so generously to it or at all as the Gentile-heavy churches of Achaia and Macedonia had done. Still, the Lord's gifts do not come according to the measure of our deserving. They come according to the measure of our need, and Paul's collection from the Gentile Christians for the Jewish Christians came likewise. In joining that collection, the Corinthians will participate in Jesus' way. They will imitate Paul's graciousness and thus imitate Christ (11:1).

2 CORINTHIANS

AUTHOR

Paul is the author (2 Corinthians 1:1).

COMPOSITION AND PURPOSE

This letter follows at a small interval from the first. In 2 Corinthians 8:10 and 9:2 Paul refers to a "year ago," which could be a full year of months between 1 Corinthians and this one or a calendar year since the Macedonian year began in September. It would be as if one wrote a letter in February, referred to a previous letter written in December, and said "When I wrote you last year," though it was only a few months earlier. Whether twelve months or fewer, the second letter intends to address some remaining confusions in the Corinthian church and to involve them more broadly in the collection for Jerusalem. Those two things will also help them understand the nature and purpose of Paul's suffering and their suffering, something the apostle addresses at the beginning and the end of this letter.

OUTLINE

1:1-11	INTRODUCTION
1:12-2:17	AFFLICTION AND DIVINE COMFORT
3:1-7:16	THE NATURE OF THE HOLY MINISTRY
8:1-9:15	CHRISTIANS GIVING FROM CHRIST'S ABUNDANCE
10:1-13:10	AN APOLOGY OF THE MINISTRY OF PAUL
13:11-14	CONCLUSION

CONNECTIONS TO THE OLD AND NEW TESTAMENTS

Isaiah and Psalms figure prominently in the letter's use of the Old Testament, as they do throughout the New Testament. The most extended single set of quotations is the chain from 6:16-18 where Paul uses verses from Leviticus, Ezekiel, Isaiah, and 2 Samuel to demonstrate the difference between God's holy people and the sons of disobedience. When a specific topic such as holiness is under discussion, this is a perfect example of how the Scriptures bring passages together from many widespread points in the Bible to address that single topic thoroughly.

There are many references back to the situation and advice of 1 Corinthians. For starters, compare 2 Corinthians 1:8 to 1 Corinthians 12:31, 2 Corinthians 4:1 to 1 Corinthians 7:25, 2 Corinthians 8:8 to 1 Corinthians 7:6, and 2 Corinthians 11:5-6 to 1 Corinthians 2:1 and 14:23. You will find the Spirit of God addressing a congregation's needs through Paul's words with clarity and directness.

CHAPTER 1

This marvelous pastoral epistle begins with Paul's suffering and ends with the Corinthians' comfort. Here, we do not see the qualifications of the ministry as much as in 1 Timothy or Titus, as the nature of the ministry — what its crosses are, what its sacrifices are, and what its glories are. Paul does not write here to potential supporters he does not know as he did to the Romans. He writes to beloved children who cause him great joy and sorrow. In all things, he writes to build them up, not tear them down.

His sufferings have been many, but not one has been without purpose. If Paul suffers, it redounds to the Corinthians' comfort and salvation (1:6). If he is comforted and his suffering relieved, this becomes a comfort to those he serves (1:7). The secret of contentment – knowing how to suffer want and how to enjoy abundance – is found in the reliance on Christ's comfort and Christ's power that Paul and his fellow workers Timothy (1:1) and Titus (7:6) have learned through affliction. If the Christian must live the life of Christ for others in 1 Corinthians, the Christian must also live the life of Christ for himself in 2 Corinthians. In his service to others and in his own life the Christian proclaims and experiences the power of God to raise the dead (1:9).[18]

The apostle's nearness to this congregation means his great desire to see them again as he travels on to Judea with the collection (1 Corinthians 16:1). However, some accuse him of being double-minded about his purpose in returning (1:17) because he wanted to spare them the pain his first letter (1 Corinthians) caused them (2 Corinthians 2:1). Their faith should not rest on whether Paul has or has not come recently but on Jesus Christ in Whom God's promises find a Yes every time (1:20). Their reliance in life must rest on Christ and no other, as in all affliction and in all giving and in everything Paul will mention in the rest of the letter.

CHAPTER 2

Paul's sorrow has been relieved through their obedience to his first letter (2:3-4). They must now ease the sorrow of the man whom they corrected (1 Corinthians 5:1-13) and who has obeyed their admonition, lest he should be overwhelmed through sorrow for sin and not know God's forgiveness through His church (2:10). If someone knows only sorrow over his sin and does not know Christ's forgiveness, Satan has an open door for his work of inciting despair in our souls. Forgiveness of the sinner is the congregation's weapon against Satan to reclaim the sinner for Christ's kingdom and purposes (2:11).

Paul recounts his travels between the last letter and this one to indicate they were not random wanderings. He has not haphazardly chosen places to go, but God, like a victorious ancient general, has led him and the whole church "in triumphal procession" (2:14) as the gospel goes through the world. Its savor is life-giving to believers and death-dealing to unbelievers (2:15-16), and its progress is according to God's command. Its advance happens through the Word of God, sincerely proclaimed by Paul, not peddled for selfish gain as so many do. To those peddlers, the apostle will return when he defends his own ministry in particular (11:1-12:21).

CHAPTER 3

What is that ministry? It is a ministry of the Holy Spirit to deliver the gospel to the world (3:3-4). The Christian ministry is not primarily an administration of the knowledge of God's law to the world, as was Moses' ministry (3:7), whose purpose was to bring the knowledge of sin and, through that knowledge, the reality of death. The Mosaic ministry was a service of death. It ensured that sinners would die for their sins, and its writing was on stone tablets to fix the letters of condemnation firmly. The Christian ministry is a service of life. It ensures that sinners will live forever through Christ's death, and its writing is on hearts to make them altogether new (3:3, 6, 10). There is an end-date on the Mosaic ministry because one day death will be no more (3:7), but the Christian ministry looks forward to everlasting life, which remains forever (3:11).

The boldness of the apostles' preaching rests on the nature of their ministry. They are

---

18 One learns from such experiences to trust more in God and to distrust one's heart more often, per 1·9 cited in Ap. VI.54.

very bold because there is no barrier between them and an unholy people, such as there was between holy Moses with his face veiled (3:13) and unholy Israel with their minds hardened through sin (3:14). They cannot even understand God's Word because when they read it, the sin that hardens them gets in the way of their understanding the Scriptures (3:15).[19] But if the Spirit comes through the preaching of the gospel, then everything opens up (3:16), and freedom replaces slavery and life supplants death.

CHAPTER 4

Such a ministry is so mighty and glorious (3:18) that there is no need to add or subtract anything from God's Word (4:2). God's Word will, alone, do everything necessary to reach the human conscience (4:2), and to change the human heart. People who do not believe the gospel will not understand the gospel and will even hate the smell of that gospel (2:16) because Satan has made them blind to God's glory in Christ (4:4). What they do not see is what Paul's gospel makes brilliantly clear: God's glory and image is in Christ Jesus. Look to Him and be saved! (4:4).

Very humble men bear such a gospel. They need not be humble in their walk, mannerisms, or anything else resembling humility without needing to be humble. They are humble in what they suffer and humble in their perplexity and humble in every circumstance of their lives (4:7-10), so that as they live the death of Jesus for others (4:10), others might live through the life of Jesus risen from the dead that they proclaim (4:11-14).

This is the outcome of the life Paul described and pleaded for the Corinthians to live in his first letter because its outcome for others is that they live through the gospel the suffering, afflicted, humble Christian proclaims. No Christian needs to rely on his humility or his prosperity. He must rely in all afflictions and all abundance on Christ, Who raises the dead. The things we can see in our lives – how much we own or how little we have, how much honor we receive, or how little we are recognized – matter very little because they all are passing away with this old world. Only Christ will bring in the new world that will abide forever, so we trust only in Him for all things now and always (4:16-18).

> 1 Timothy, 2 Timothy, and Titus are usually called the Pastoral Epistles as a group. 2 Corinthians discusses the reason and nature of the office of the ministry at some length (chapters 1-4) but is not reckoned with them. Why? Much of how we organize the Bible in our minds is based on traditional labels – the Pastoral Epistles, the Synoptic Gospels, the Minor Prophets, for example – that have their reasons but also their blind spots. The adventure of studying Scripture is finding the Spirit-wrought connections between 2 Corinthians and 2 Timothy or Amos and 1 Kings that manmade labels perhaps obscured. 2 Corinthians is a pastoral epistle because it displays what the pastoral ministry is, not because any Bible publisher labeled it that way. The words of Scripture matter more than the labels publishers assign to them.

CHAPTER 5

Since this world is passing away, we now have more of a tent than a mansion. Paul does not mean this to say that the human body is a shell that will one day be cast off so that the soul

---

19 Ap. III.13 further defines the veil of 3:15 as "the human opinion concerning the entire Law, the Decalog, and the ceremonies, namely, that hypocrites think that external and civil works satisfy the Law of God and that sacrifices and observances justify before God."

may fly away free from the body, as many today believe. Instead, he speaks of a transformation of lowly things into wondrous things, as he also spoke of in 1 Corinthians 15 about the resurrection of the flesh. Now we suffer in this body, but Christ will transform our lowly bodies to be like His glorious Body, even as He is now transforming our suffering to serve the comfort of others (1:6). If we die before His return, we indeed are "absent from the body" (5:8) and at home with Him. Still, we await the day of His judgment seat (5:10) when we receive His righteous judgment (John 5:29).

Since we must appear before Christ and before no other, we fear Him and do all things for His sake. Paul is not afraid to seem insane to the Corinthians (5:13) if it means that he is doing everything possible to get the gospel of Christ into the consciences of his fellow men (5:11). Any minister who seeks a good opinion from everyone and not to commend himself to everyone's conscience through preaching (5:12) is unfaithful and is seeking recognition in the flesh (5:16), that is, the very kind of recognition the Lord Himself did not receive in His ministry (5:16). Rather, everyone should be regarded as a new creation through Christ (5:17) so that someone's appearance matters not at all and his adherence to Christ matters above all.

For Christ's own adherence to God's Word is the church's message of reconciliation: God did not count our real trespasses against us but made Christ to be a sin-offering (5:21) on our behalf so that we might be reconciled to God through Christ's sacrifice. The minister is God's ambassador to announce His satisfaction with Christ's work and His mercy toward sinners forgiven solely for Christ's work (5:20). The minister has nothing else to do than to announce that work and herald that forgiveness and to put not his own appearance but Christ the image of God before the people's eyes.

Chapter 6

Paul's self-sacrifice (6:4-5) and the lengths he has gone to for the sake of the Corinthians (6:6-10) are solely because the gospel is always urgent. The best day to believe is always today. Tomorrow is not guaranteed. Putting one's preferences aside, which he gave so much time in 1 Corinthians 8:1-11:1 (and compare 6:3 here), is the method of a man in a hurry who cannot wait for people to adjust to his demands. Instead, he lives with an open heart, eager for his hearers to believe (6:11) so that God's power might rest on them, too, and they might all live in Him.

The Corinthians must understand, then, that light, trifling things have not been set aside for their sake, as ungrateful children imagine their parents have made no sacrifices for them and do not really love them (6:12). They must know how great the sacrifices are that were made for them so they may be God's temple and belong to Him and not trifle with the things of this world, which are really the devil's things (6:15). They are not members of a social club. They are God's own dwelling (6:15), God's holy people (6:16), and God's family (6:18).

Chapter 7

Holiness and the demand to be holy have produced a good sorrow like the repentant man of 2 Corinthians 2. They have all heeded what Paul told them in his first letter, which was shortly thereafter accompanied by a visit from Paul's coworker, Titus. If he sent Timothy with his first letter to their repentant sorrow (1 Corinthians 4), Titus' visit has been the proof of their earnestness to amend their ways (7:11-13). The list of the marks of earnestness – indignation, fear, longing, zeal, avenging of wrong (7:11) – lists all the things their pride and boasting did not display before the apostle wrote his first letter to them. In hearing God's Word, they must become and have become different people and a different congregation than they were before.

Paul is happy to boast, but since he who boasts must boast in the Lord, Paul has boasted in the Lord's children at Corinth to Titus (7:14). He was confident, and his confidence was proven correct that God's children listen to God's Word and heed His voice, cause for great rejoicing by the proud father, Paul (7:16). Congregations are changed through the open, honest preaching of God's Word, and the minister has only his own cowardice to blame if he shrinks back from declaring to God's people the whole counsel of God's Word (Acts 20:27).

Chapter 8

A congregation freshly engaged with God's Word is ready to be freshly engaged with the ministry of His gospel to every nation. Paul is eager to have the Corinthians join in the collection for Jerusalem, already so successful in the impoverished churches of the province of Macedonia (8:1). Though those congregations are quite poor, they gave above and beyond their ability (8:3). Titus will be the agent of helping the Corinthians likewise to surpass expectation and to provide abundantly for the sake of God's people as Christ gave Himself abundantly for the poor (8:9). Christian giving is the mirror of Christ's self-giving: above and beyond for the other's sake.

Such giving is profitable not for someone's accounting but for the souls of the givers (8:10) because all the abundance flows from God to His people for all of His people, just as the manna was given in such measure that everyone had enough (8:15). All His gifts are given to all of His people so that they could share and supply one another's need. Titus and all the ministers of the churches are there to ensure that God's manna is spread around so that all Israel may feast on His gifts.

Chapter 9

Paul sent the "messengers of the churches" (8:23) to ensure that the Corinthians would be ready to give to the Jerusalem collection, as he knows they are. Yet, like the obedience of Philemon to Paul's plea for the slave Onesimus, the apostle does not desire a forced gift. Instead, he insists on three principles in a Christian's giving: 1) abundance leads to abundance; the more that is sown, the more that is reaped in the harvest (9:6); 2) each must give according to his own determination so his giving is cheerful and ready rather than a forced tax (9:7); and 3) God will supply all that is lacking for anyone (9:8-11).

Notice that God's abundant supply will suffice for the Corinthians, for Jerusalem, and all. Any gift from the Corinthians will be to their credit and with thanksgiving to God (9:13, 15), but God will supply all that anyone needs. There is no question that His will shall be done, and His people will be fed and given all they need in His service. The only question is whether and how and how much the Corinthians will enter into the service of His gifts to His people. He does not need us to give gifts. We need Him to be givers of gifts ourselves.

> Under discussion in 2 Corinthians 8-9 is the Corinthians' participation in the collection Paul has organized for the Jewish Christians in Jerusalem. Those gifts of money are meant for sharing as surely as the gifts Paul described in 1 Corinthians 12-14. Some gifts are useful for the local congregation, such as prophesying or administration, and some for the broader church because things like money can be transported to help far away. All gifts are meant for the whole body of Christ to be built up, whether with us in the congregation on the Lord's Day or far from us in body but close to us in the Spirit of God.

Chapter 10

Paul's impending visit to the Corinthians causes them uncertainty about how he will be with them when they meet. He is clear that his ministry is not in opposition to anyone because his warfare is not against human flesh and blood (10:3) but against spiritual foes fought using God's Spirit. So, the authority that Paul has is the authority to tear down everything opposed to the knowledge of God (10:5) and the authority to enslave all thoughts in obedience to Christ. They need fear nothing from the minister of God because he will not come to tear them down or to enslave them to himself. He will come to magnify Christ, even as he would have Christ's gospel preached with their help throughout all nations (10:16).

This understanding of authority and later of boasting (10:13-18) anchors the ministry in the use of the Word of God to put to flight the enemies of God. It is never hostility to any human being because it is not carried on according to the flesh (10:3). Rather, the ministry uses the Word of God to destroy falsehood and to inculcate truth. Those who boast in any other means or methods of ministry boast in themselves, not in the Lord, Who casts down His enemies from their false thrones through the preaching of His Word.

Chapter 11

This extended defense of Paul's ministry, recounting his method of supporting himself in the congregation's earliest days (11:8) and displaying the intense emotion of a church planter toward the congregation he planted (11:11, 18-21), is the defense love makes when its truthfulness is challenged. Do you really love someone? Prove it. Paul's proof is that he has lived toward the Corinthians as Christ lived toward him: loving the unlovable, making the poor rich, giving himself to the utmost.

This has not prevented the Corinthians from falling in love like the Galatians with other preachers who proclaim themselves and not Christ. Such preachers boast in the law of Moses as if it were not a "ministry of death" (3:7) and as if their sufficiency came from Moses rather than Christ. Paul is willing to play that game as a pretense of insanity and believes he would be victorious if we measured our lives according to our devotion to the law of Moses or our productivity in the church's work (11:22-29).

These are no grounds for a Christian to boast because such claims are not grounded in Christ. Instead, Paul boasts in his weakness because his weakness is where Christ's power is made known. In his weakness, Christ becomes his whole strength, and even when kings threaten him, Christ is mighty to deliver (11:32-33). Life in Christ is life from Christ's hand, a life of confidence in Christ, not in oneself or one's qualifications or achievements, whether real or pretended.

Chapter 12

The visionary experience Paul relates (12:1-6) is much like John's in Revelation (Revelation 1:10), but while the Spirit of God preserved John's vision as He did also the visions of many Old Testament prophets, what Paul saw was given only to Paul to see (12:2) and not for us to know. Paul could look at that with a sense of strangeness or regret, but he understands God's purpose in showing him the things he saw to be in service for the rest of his life.

The visions were not some wonderful exception to a dreary life. They relate directly to the suffering Paul undergoes constantly, his "thorn in the flesh" (12:7) that keeps him from being puffed up by the knowledge of his visions and torments him continually. What was the thorn?

Many strange theories exist about its nature. Since he mentions all this while discussing his opponents, the "super-apostles" (12:11), who dog him everywhere he goes, promoting the law of Moses and the gospel of Christ, it seems most straightforward and clearest to understand his opponents as his thorn. Wherever the gospel goes, the opponents go to pervert it. Wherever Paul preaches, the opponents follow with their version of things.

Why would God allow this to happen? Paul has done and does everything to build up the Corinthians (12:19), and the danger is constant that they will fall away from the one gospel of Christ that Paul preaches and slide into the weaknesses of the flesh that false gospels always indulge (12:20-21). That indulgence has caused the errors and unclean practices mentioned in 12:21 to grow so much that the first letter to the Corinthians was necessary. What if all his preaching has been in vain since they easily fall under the opponents' sway into these lies? Christ's assurance in words recorded by God's Spirit but not recorded in one of the four gospels is that "My grace is sufficient for you" (12:9)[20] so that even the mighty preacher of Christ, Paul, must rely throughout his ministry and in every circumstance and congregation on Christ's power to preserve His church, not on Paul's power to hold it all together. Finally, Christ must rule the church despite all appearances, and Paul's ability to keep things on track must be revealed as no ability at all. All ability, power, and dominion over and in the church belong to King Jesus. Only He can, and only He does rule His Body, for when we are weak, just then He is strong (12:10).

Chapter 13

There was a time when even our King was weak (13:4). Still, now, in our weakness and since His resurrection, He is mighty (12:3). There is no sense in testing Paul as if he had to answer to the tests of his opponents (12:2-3) because Paul's proof of the ministry is not in himself but in the proclamation of the mighty Christ (12:5). Jesus Christ is in the church's midst through His Word. The question is not whether Paul should be an apostle but whether a church turning against God's Word can still be considered a church (13:5).

Just as the careless eating of the Lord's Supper degenerated into munching and guzzling that was no Lord's Supper at all in Corinth (1 Corinthians 11:20), a Corinthian congregation or any congregation that does not recognize Christ in their midst through His gospel (summed up in 13:4) is no congregation at all. In this second letter, the Corinthians are enamored of false teachers and in danger of forsaking everything, as were the Galatians (Galatians 1:7-8). This letter is sternly written with a wide-open heart only a father could have for his children (13:10-11) to keep his children in the faith, to defend the ministry he has carried out in their midst, and to magnify Christ's glory to a people half in love with every form of fleshly glory (11:19-20).

---

[20] The worthiness of Christians who are "of weak faith, diffident, troubled, and heartily terrified because of the greatness and number of their sins" (FC SD VII.69) at Christ's altar is emphasized on the basis of 12.9.

GALATIANS

AUTHOR

Paul is the author (Galatians 1:1).

COMPOSITION AND PURPOSE

The intended destination of the "churches of Galatia" (1:2) could be either all the churches in the area in the mountains of central Anatolia, also known as North Galatia for the Celts who had overrun the district, or they are the residents of the churches in the southern part of the Roman province of Galatia, where we know Paul visited and brought a collection to Jerusalem (see Acts 20:4 and following). Paul may have addressed either or both. Neither part of the province of Galatia may be excluded without a doubt because Paul uses the names of Roman provinces, not of districts such as Ancyra (North Galatia). Anywhere inside the Roman province of Galatia could be where his letter was sent.

Some believe that he sent the letter before the council of Jerusalem in Acts 15, some after that meeting, and some are unsure. All such guesses rely on many other guesses in a given scholar's thinking, and guesses are just that and that only. We cannot place the letter's date definitely because the problems with the circumcision party existed throughout Paul's ministry. The likeliest scenario is that Galatians 2 is Paul's story of Acts 15 and that the letter follows that council despite its rulings about the validity of Paul's mission to the Gentiles. The apostle must turn the Galatians back to the clarity and fullness of the gospel because they are troubled by things that the council in Jerusalem was supposed to have resolved.

OUTLINE

1:1-5	GREETING (WITHOUT THANKSGIVING)
1:6-10	CURSE PRONOUNCED ON THOSE UNFAITHFUL TO THE GOSPEL
1:11-2:21	PAUL'S CONDUCT TO PRESERVE THE GOSPEL
3:1-4:31	GOD'S PROMISE AND THE PLACE OF THE LAW
5:1-6:10	LIFE ACCORDING TO THE SPIRIT AND NOT ACCORDING TO THE FLESH
6:11-18	CONCLUSION

CONNECTIONS TO THE OLD AND NEW TESTAMENTS

Galatians has extensive overlap with the letter to the Romans since, in both places, the basics of Paul's preaching are in question. It also shares James' interest in the justification of Abraham (see James 2:20-26) and the inheritance that comes through the promises made to him. It is particularly rich through discussion of Abraham's life and Paul's allegory in Galatians 4:21-31 in the interpretation of Genesis and the significance of the promise given to Abraham concerning his Seed, Christ Jesus, preceding the law given to Moses (3:17) by centuries.

Chapter 1

The apostle begins with urgency, not stopping even to give thanks for the church of Galatia because it is in danger of death. A church without the gospel is no church at all, and the doctor cannot stop to introduce himself with pleasantries when the patient is about to die. He must act quickly to stop the bleeding; there will be enough time for niceties afterward.

How did it come to this? How does a church fall away from Christ entirely? It is not a certain quantity of moral failings or laxness that has brought the Galatians to this pass. The Corinthians seem to have enough moral problems and strange practices to spare, yet Paul can give thanks for their faith. The Galatians are in danger not of this or that error, this or that oddity. They are in danger of not being Christians at all anymore because they do not trust in the death of Christ for their salvation.

Paul stresses his calling because in proving that his calling from directly from Christ, he can prove that the gospel he preaches is also directly from Christ without a mediator such as the law had (3:19). His gospel does not require being near Jerusalem (1:17) or consulting with church authorities about what he should preach (see 1:19). His gospel came when Christ revealed Himself to Paul on the Damascus road (Acts 9) so that Paul abandoned Judaism (1:14) and trusted Christ and proclaimed Christ also to the Gentiles throughout many regions of the Near East (1:17-18, 21). Not an iota of that proclamation had to do with authorization by some other power or authority than Jesus Christ and His gospel.

Chapter 2

The consultation in 2:1-2, 8-9 that made Paul go to Jerusalem to lay out his gospel is likely the meeting of Acts 15. However, the controversy over the law and circumcision is broad enough that there could have been multiple meetings on the same subject. Whether Paul went to Jerusalem many times to relate his ministry and to find agreement with other apostles that God sent messengers to the Jews and the Gentiles (2:9) or whether he went one time as narrated in Acts, the problem is the same: circumcision or being legally Jewish or otherwise qualifying to be near God in Christ through the law are all utterly vain, which is why Titus was not even circumcised on the trip to Jerusalem (2:3).

Those who are troubling the church are "false brothers" (2:4) because they pretend to be in Christ with Jews and Gentiles but cannot abide the freedom that Jew and Gentile have in Christ through faith only. Paul is very firm on this point, and this accusation (2:5) because to yield on this would be to give up the gospel and to become obsessed with manmade status (2:6), something that only becomes important if, for instance, being

Jewish is reckoned as somehow better than being Gentile according to the law as the false brothers teach.

> Many believe that the church faces its greatest dangers from outside opposition to the gospel, but the testimony of this letter along with many other portions of Scripture is that the greatest destruction is done from within the church. Judas arose against Christ from within the Twelve, and from within his own priestly family, Moses found Aaron leading Israel into idolatry. The world is opposed to Christ and does not know Him, but the gospel's greatest enemies always originate from within the household of God.

Peter's cowardice (Paul usually calls him "Cephas") was to be free to eat with Gentiles when only Gentiles were around and to lose the courage of his convictions about the gospel when his fellow Jews were around. He reverted to Jewish food laws and the exclusion of Gentiles from meals and social occasions when fellow Jews came who still looked on Gentile Christians as "sinners" (2:15) as Paul and Peter had been raised to despise them for being. Peter's hypocrisy is bad enough, even as other Jews imitate it in the church (2:13), but it is nonsensical too. Peter did for himself what the Galatians are doing as Paul writes to them: deserting the gospel with its freedom to associate with Jew or Gentile for a return to the law of Moses that will enslave all to keep all of it once more. This is a vain hope because the law cannot justify any sinner. No sinner can get the perfect score required by the law, and therefore, any justified sinner must and can only be justified by faith in Christ (2:16).

This justification by faith is also a crucifixion with Christ so that through faith, one dies to the claims of the law, and to the ways of life those claims stir up in the false brothers and in Peter. One dies by faith in Christ to any notion that anything other than Christ is needed for salvation. If the law could do the things the false brothers teach it can do or the things Peter has once more begun to act like it can do, then there would be no need for Christ to die. Why would He do that if we could get the same result through our works? It would have been pointless if the law could do what Paul's opponents claim it can do. False teaching about the law always makes Christ pointless to the Christian and the church; that is why such teaching is a desertion of the gospel.

Chapter 3

Paul speaks to the Galatians as if they have fallen under the evil eye (Matthew 6:23), a curse that causes them to think such stupid things as salvation through works of the law. The problem with the law is that it does not bring God's Spirit or His holiness. Perfection cannot be achieved through the law, and the suffering in Christ that the Galatians have already experienced (3:4) is pointless if the law could have perfected them. They would not have needed any of Christ's Spirit or Christ's suffering, the sort that Paul himself suffers (6:17), if the law and the flesh that it stirs up could work together for their salvation.

By the law, they are trying to gain something Scripture has not promised to the doers of the law. Scripture promised that those who have Abraham's blessings, the true sons of Abraham that many in that time wanted to be (see Matthew 3:9) are those who have faith in God's promises. The true division among mankind is not between Jew and Gentile. It is between those of faith and those of the law. Those of faith are blessed (3:6-9), and those of the law are accursed and do not find life (3:10). The righteous live only by faith (Habakkuk 2:4 and Galatians 3:11). Christ ended the law's power over our lives – a power driving to endless death – through His own death (3:13), so that the Gentiles would receive life and His Spirit through faith in Him (3:14).[21]

The Scriptures always laid these things out. This is no private opinion of Paul's or some novelty of the Reformation. 430 years before the giving of the law on Mount Sinai through the hands of angels to Moses, Abraham was promised that his Seed would be blessed and all blessed in Him (3:16). The Scripture is clear that that singular Seed is Jesus Christ, through Whom we all become God's sons and heirs of all His promises (3:26-27). So mighty is this promise that one's ethnicity, free or slave status, and sex, things Paul addresses in other places to discuss vocation, do not matter at all in the gospel because, by faith, we are all in Christ and have everything coming to us that is His, Abraham's Seed, all His righteousness, all His victory, all His life, whether we are Russian or Japanese, slave or free, male or female. All that counts is faith in Christ.

The law cannot do those things because God did not give it to Moses to do those things. It was not and cannot be the promised Savior. The law was given to mankind to drive us like a tutor walked his young charges to school or like a bus driver drives children to school so that we could get to Christ (3:23-24). The law makes sin exceedingly clear so that we are all imprisoned in the same prison of the law that Christ might come and free us by faith (3:22). To use the law as a means of salvation is to use it wrongly or unlawfully, as Paul explains in other places (1 Timothy 1:8).

Chapter 4

Life under the law is slavery. The slavery to "elementary principles" (4:3) or "those which by nature are no gods" (4:8) shows that life under the law is natural to fallen man since all peoples everywhere adhere to the teachings of demons until and unless Christ claims them as His own through the preaching of the gospel. The gospel frees us from our native slavery and makes us sons of God who cry out to our Father (4:6).

This makes the Galatians' desertion so strange. Who, after his emancipation, wishes to return to slavery? They have even begun to despise Paul, whom they once received as an angel of God (4:14) because he brought them the knowledge of the true God and formed Christ in them through his preaching (compare 4:19).

Paul creates an allegory – an extended comparison or metaphor – using the figures of Sarah and Hagar because Isaac was born freely from Sarah according to God's promise, and Ishmael was born in slavery according to the will of the flesh. His allegory goes further to identify Isaac with the heavenly Jerusalem, the mother of Christians, the church, the place that God dwells with man in peace (4:26), and Ishmael with the

---

21 The Holy Spirit is only received through faith (Ap. III.6), and the Law does not give the power and ability to begin and do a new life, as the only the Holy Spirit coming through the preaching of the gospel can renew the heart (FC SD VI.11-12).

earthly Jerusalem, the source of the false brothers, the troubler of the church, the place where man is enslaved through the law, much like Mount Sinai (4:24-25). Only one of these two boys inherits Abraham's promises and blessings, and it is the son of the free woman, Sarah's boy, who lives by promise (4:28), just as all Christians live by faith in God's promise.

Chapter 5

Christ died to free us. His death is our emancipation, but if we put ourselves under the law, we cannot use His death or blood to our credit and must make up the whole debt of our sin on our own. Such attempted justification by the law is severance from Christ's body (5:4) as if we were once His members but had been amputated. Paul wishes that those teaching justification by the law would amputate their own members (5:12) since they are so eager for the circumcision of the Gentiles (5:3). If circumcision were all that mattered, Paul would not be persecuted, but he is indeed persecuted still because sinners do not hate the law. They hate the cross, and the Christ crucified upon it and persecute His messengers (5:11).

The exhortation to walk in the Spirit is now given (5:25) because Isaac and Ishmael, the free man and the slave, each have their own ways of life. The Spirit has a certain way that we follow by faith in Christ, and the flesh has its way that we can follow through the law. The irony of the law is that when you set your heart to keep all of it all the time, you indulge your flesh (4:17, 19), which the law seizes. It knows the law condemns sin and makes sin very clear, and the flesh uses that clarity to practice sin greedily more. The Spirit does not do that. Through faith, we have died with Christ and crucified our flesh with its greedy passions and desires (5:24). Now, we walk in the Spirit's freedom, bearing the Spirit's fruit in Christ (5:22-23). The only way to destroy sin and to live a holy life is through the Spirit by faith in Christ.

Chapter 6

Gentleness, carrying one another's burdens, and refusing to boast in oneself all come from the Holy Spirit since the flesh loves harshness with others, refuses to bear another's burden, and loud boasting about one's accomplishments. Generous giving, especially to the ministers of the gospel for their work, has that abundance that God's Spirit Himself possesses and creates in those walking in step with Him (compare 5:25 to 6:8-10). Such spiritual people do not bite and devour one another as do the adherents of the circumcision and the law.

Those adherents do not themselves actually keep the law, as Peter also did not keep the law to which he held the Gentiles (2:14, 6:13). Their purpose in promoting the law rather than faith is that the law gives people a reason for boasting in themselves (6:14)[22] and prevents such false brothers from being persecuted for the sake of Christ (6:12).

---

22 The old Adam is disciplined by the law's admonition and threats as well as "punishments and blows, so that he may follow and surrender himself captive to the Spirit," citing this verse among others in Fc Ep VI.4.

Such law-driven preachers need no cross of Christ and so are never persecuted because of or like that crucified Christ. A crucified Christ is always too much trouble for the adherents of the law to bother with. A crucified Christ is peace and mercy (6:16) to all who receive Him and His benefits solely by faith.

Time proves all things. With time, it will be known whether this or that preacher's work has been worthwhile, like silver or gold or fruitless and flimsy like a building made of wood, hay, or straw (3:12).[23] For now, that matters little because the focus must be on what God says and how God builds since the Corinthians are His field, His building, not Paul's (3:9). They are a new temple (3:16-17) and must be built up according to God's instructions as the old temple was. Christians may be indifferent to whether there is a temple in Jerusalem as there was then. God is done with physical buildings built by human hands. Instead, he is building a spiritual building built by the word of the cross among all nations. Boasting about this or that preacher is as foolish as boasting in Solomon or Bezalel in the temple of old. What matters is that God is dwelling with men, that we belong to Christ, and that Christ, through His cross and resurrection, belongs to God (3:23).

EPHESIANS

AUTHOR

The writer is Paul (1:1).

COMPOSITION AND PURPOSE

The letter was written during Paul's captivity in Caesarea or Rome around the same time as the letter to the Colossians. That puts the letter in the very late 50s or early 60s AD before Paul's ministry was finished in his martyrdom in Rome around 64 AD. He wants the church in Ephesus to grasp what it is and how it can endure once he is gone, though he has been so central to it its whole life until then.

OUTLINE

1:1-23	GREETING OF THE CHURCH AND PRAISE OF GOD
2:1-22	THE NATURE AND POWER OF OUR SALVATION

---

23 The rewards for building well are clearly delineated on the basis of 3-8 in Ap. III.244, "…although justification and eternal life pertain to faith, nevertheless good works merit other bodily and spiritual rewards and degrees of rewards."

3:1-21	THE NATURE AND POWER OF THE MINISTRY OF SALVATION
4:1-16	THE NATURE AND PURPOSE OF GIFTS
4:17-32	THE LIFE OF DARKNESS AND LIFE IN THE LIGHT
5:1-21	ON UNFRUITFUL AND FRUITFUL WORKS
5:22-6:9	HOUSEHOLD INSTRUCTIONS
6:10-17	WARFARE UPON THE POWERS
6:18-24	FAREWELL

CONNECTIONS TO THE OLD AND NEW TESTAMENTS

Direct quotations from the Old Testament come from Psalms (mostly) and once each from Zechariah, Genesis, and Exodus. The imagery of the church as the dwelling place of the Holy Spirit relies on the reader or hearer's knowledge of the Jerusalem temple and the filling of that temple with God's glory to see how beautiful is God's church filled with His Spirit.

In its clear discussion of the nature of the church and how Christ cares for His Bride, Ephesians has a close cousin in the letter to the Colossians that was written around the same time in Paul's imprisonment. It also shares the sense of saying goodbye that we hear in 2 Timothy, another captivity letter, and Paul's expression of his legacy in the churches. In the beauty of its language, it gives place perhaps only to the letter to the Hebrews for its majesty and power.

CHAPTER 1

From prison, the apostle writes to strengthen the church at Ephesus in their sufferings and blessings. He would have them know how precious they are to Christ since the church is the dwelling place of His Holy Spirit, the very temple of God. Whatever happens to him or them, they have every blessing already in Christ Who is seated at the Father's right hand and rules for the benefit of His own Body, the holy church.

The church is where God's mysteries hidden for long ages are made known – His predestination of us for adoption as His sons, the nature of His Son's work on our behalf, the incorporation of the Gentiles into the Israel of God. In the church, light shines on darkness, and what was unclear in the Scriptures, such as the eventual conversion of the Gentiles, becomes apparent through the proclamation of divine truth.

This is why the whole chapter from v. 3 onward is a benediction or blessing of God for His glories and His mercies. Paul's story of how he and the other apostles came to the faith (1:4-12) and then communicated that faith to the Ephesians (1:13-14) and how the Ephesians now grow in the knowledge of God and faith in Christ (1:15-23) is a story of God's blessings in Christ moving from something unknown to something known, from a hidden place in His fatherly heart to the open preaching of these glorious truths in the church for the sake of the whole world. For such wonders, the apostle blesses the merciful Father Who has adopted us as sons from before the foundation of the world. All He purposed in that fatherly heart is freely and openly known through the gospel.

CHAPTER 2

Since the purpose and the plan were His, the initiative and the action must also be all His. The gospel must depend on the riches of His mercy (2:4) and never on our own works (2:9) so that our boasting may be in the Lord Who shows mercy and not in ourselves, since all are "by nature children of wrath," (2:3), whether born Jewish or born Gentile. Man, whether Jew or Gentile, in his sinful nature, is "dead" (2:5) in his transgressions, whether he is circumcised or not. Paul's gospel is a gospel apart from the boasting in the flesh that his opponents loved to do because, in his gospel, all men are "sons of disobedience" by nature (2:2) and become sons of God only by grace (2:8).[24]

The hostility between Jew and Gentile, symbolized by the partition of Jew from Gentile in the Jerusalem temple to which Paul refers in 2:14, is one example of the alienation of Gentiles from God's promises (2:11) and of Jews from God's promises through the inability of circumcision to save, which is the inability of the law to save sinners (2:11). Christ made satisfaction in the flesh for the law's demands (2:15) so that Jew and Gentile could have peace with one another through Him, since only His blood avails for peace with God, not circumcision or uncircumcision (2:14, 16-18). In Christ there is only one household of God or temple of God, and that is His holy people who have His Holy Spirit, built on the foundation of the words of the apostles and prophets (2:20).

CHAPTER 3

Paul's sufferings were far more significant to him than they often are to us today, just as the inclusion of the Gentiles in God's mercy was far more significant to him then than it is to us today. We do not wonder at a largely Gentile church because we are accustomed to it for almost millennia now. Paul's wonder is that God's plan has been worked out so magnificently and widely that through Christ even the nations that did not know Him now magnify His Name through faith in Christ. To grasp his wonder, you must imagine the hardest-hearted, most stubborn sinner you know coming to faith one day, and you would have some small sense of how great and how mighty His power is to save sinful mankind, even entire groups of people you would never have imagined would trust in His salvation, a fact now proclaimed in His church (3:9-10).

His sufferings are likewise significant to him because they signal his being in Christ. His prayer for similar power to withstand all and to stand firm, which he makes for the Ephesians (3:14-21), is a prayer for them to become like him in experiencing the power of God to save, heal, and bless. It is a prayer for them to live as he lives – in Christ. In Christ, one experiences the power of the love of Christ (3:18-19) more and more, and without suffering, that is, without experience of our own weakness, that love remains a small thing. Through our suffering, His power is magnified because when we are weak, He is strong. Paul asks that blessing for the church as he has himself been blessed in his own weakness.

CHAPTER 4

The life in Christ has a goal. It is never static because through Christ the entire church is growing up. The image of God in Christ is the measure of our full maturity (4:13). We do not all

---

24 The exclusive particles (usually cited in the Confessions in the Latin as particulae exclusivae) in Paul's discussions of justification as in 2-8 are there to "urge with special diligence…by which the merit of Christ is entirely separated from our works," FC Ep. III.10.

have the same tasks in the church because some are in the ministry (4:11), and some are built up through that ministry for their own callings (4:12-13), but we are all called to maturity in Christ (4:14-16), that stability and wisdom that come from the body's growth from frail childhood into sturdy manhood. All this flows from the gifts Christ is eager to give in His church (4:11) and through His church (4:16) because His ascension has won for that church, His Body, everything that it could possibly need (4:8).

Of those gifts, Paul exhorts the church to take advantage and not turn as the sinful man is wont to turn (Romans 7) back to the love of his own flesh. The church cannot live like the world lives because the world – here called Gentiles because they are without God, not because of their ethnicity as opposed to the church that has Jews and Gentiles in it – is opposed to God, hardhearted, callous, and greedy to defile itself (4:17-19). The Christians learned from Paul and others a different way of life, Christ's way (4:20-21), which means putting off one's old sinful self (4:22) and being renewed in our speech (4:25, 29), our emotions (4:26, 31-32), our use of time (4:28),[25] and how we consider other people (4:25-32) so that Christ's way is our way in the church since we are His Body, His Bride.

Chapter 5

That Bride is one flesh with her Lord, so we are "imitators" (5:1), beloved children since our Lord and Bridegroom is the beloved Son. That marriage has a negative aspect and a positive one. We avoid the talk and the life that signal we love our sin, which is idolatry (5:2-5). Some, even in the church, may want to convince us that such sin is a light thing (5:6), but Paul is clear that God's wrath is manifest – open and self-evident – upon the world, the "sons of disobedience" (2:2, 5:6) because of their greediness to talk and to live against God's will. We cannot share in the world's ways unless we want to share the world's condemnation. Its unfruitful darkness (5:11) is unlike the light we have received through Christ (5:8), to which we awake afresh whenever we heed God's Word (5:14-15). Songs of Christ awaken us to life instead of alcohol lulling us into sleepy numbness (5:18-19).

> Marriage is a vital concern of the church because it reflects the relationship between Christ and His church. If that cannot be seen, it is hard to see how Christ and the church should relate to one another, with the Head caring for His Body and the Body submitting to the Head. The destruction of marriage or its abolition, as some communist societies have attempted, is an assault on Christ and on His Church. Where marriage is honored as the apostle directs, Christ may likewise be honored. Where marriage is despised, Christ is always also despised.

The chapter's admonitions about marriage are entirely uncontroversial for Christians and altogether impossible for the sons of disobedience because only the son of God knows that God's will is always best. It is always best that the woman should be loved as Christ loves His church, even if it means the sacrifice of the man's life for his bride, his own flesh, his dearest one (5:29). It is always best that the man has the respect and submission that are due him as the head of the family, just as Christ is the Head of the Church (5:23-24).

That order is blessed in time between man and woman (5:33) and in eternity between Christ and His Church (5:31-32). The world does not recognize a blessing in time or eternity because it does not know Christ. Anyone who is in Christ finds these words comforting and clear and beautiful so that our families live in the fullness of the blessing of Jesus and His Church, loving and being loved, respecting and being respected, in submission to God's will for our eternal good in Christ (5:26-27).

Chapter 6

Children, slaves, and masters live under the same orders that wives and husbands do because God sets up life in different spheres so that each sphere has someone in authority (a husband, a parent, a master) and someone under authority (a wife, a child, a slave). The one in authority blesses the one under authority with care and love and the remembrance that all authority is accountable to God for its own actions (see 5:25, 6:4, 6:9). Through authority, God organizes His creation and blesses His creatures. Without authority, life is chaotic and a war of all against all – woman against man, child against parent, slave against master. The Scriptures envision and teach a life in and under all sorts of authority depending on one's sex, age, position, and many other factors, just as Luther summarizes in the Table of Duties.

Those varied positions all have in common the need for the whole church – male and female, old and young, slave and free - to put on God's armor against Satan's assaults. The majority of this chapter is devoted to warfare against Satan through God's Word (6:17) because in the face of Satan's rage and the world's opposition, it is possible even an apostle should be afraid to speak. Even an apostle needs the church's prayers (6:19) to proclaim the truth of Christ as he ought to do. The means for the Christians to withstand Satan's assaults are all those virtues and powers the Word of God brings us – righteousness, faith, salvation, truth, and the all the rest. The Christian is fully equipped and the church fully readied and the apostle's mouth prepared by the same, one means – the Word of God.

PHILIPPIANS

AUTHOR

Paul writes from his captivity (Philippians 1:7, 13, 16).

COMPOSITION AND PURPOSE

Out of concern for the apostle's imprisonment, the Philippian church sent Epaphroditus (2:25). Paul is now thanking the church and returning Epaphroditus to them with his love (2:25, 4:18) and perhaps Timothy his beloved child as an extra measure of his thanks for their love and care (2:19). This is the source of the letter's tremendous warmth and joy even in Paul's circumstance of imprisonment and his expectation of death (1:21-30). Bundled with the other captivity letters, it dates to Paul's imprisonment, perhaps in Caesarea or later in Rome, to the late 50s or early 60s.

OUTLINE

1:1-11	Greeting, thanksgiving, and intercession for Philippi
1:12-26	The circumstances of the apostle's life and possible death
1:27-2:18	Exhortations to endure
2:19-30	The praise of true ministers Timothy and Epaphroditus
3:1-4:1	Warnings against false teachers
4:2-9	Exhortation to unity
4:10-20	Thanksgiving for gifts
4:21-23	Farewell

CONNECTIONS TO THE OLD AND NEW TESTAMENTS

Possibly because it is a very occasional letter written because the Philippians sent Epaphroditus to look after Paul in his sickness, Philippians does not have direct quotations of the Old Testament. Its connections are indirect, so if one knows what a "generation" is in the Scriptures (see 2:15), one will see how often such generations are "crooked and perverse," as Paul describes them in this letter. It shares themes of resurrection, facing death, and focusing on the worthwhile and leaving fruitless things behind with the other captivity letters.

CHAPTER 1

Near life's end, the apostle is full of thanksgiving. This letter to the church at Philippi is a letter of giving thanks to the chief sacrifice of God's royal priesthood. In his imprisonment and suffering, Paul finds joy and gives thanks for the unbounded power of Christ to spread His Word and raise His people from the dead. On the verge of death, thanksgiving rings out still.

The apostle's and the Philippians' ends are in view. He desires that they understand how Christ is preparing them through His Word for His Day (1:10) when He will harvest the "fruit of righteousness" (1:11) with which they're filled. Adversity will be helpful to them as it has been helpful to Paul. His imprisonment spread the knowledge of the gospel to all of Caesar's own regiment, the Praetorian Guard (1:13), and this created much greater courage to speak God's Word throughout the church in Rome.

The afflictions of God's enemies become blessings to God's people, and the petty jealousies within the church cause some preachers to try to outdo Paul, who has only spread the gospel that much more widely. In all things, Christ is supreme and working all afflictions, petty jealousies, and hardships for the good of His body, the church. This is why Paul can look death in the face and say, "For me to die is gain" (1:21). He would rather die and immediately be with Christ in his spirit as all believers are (1:23), but if he remains alive, he will have fruitful labor in Christ's vineyard ahead of him still. The reason for constant thanksgiving is Christ's constant goodness through, despite, and by means of the crosses we have and the afflictions we must bear. His strength is made perfect in our weakness, and His gospel is magnified through His people's suffering (1:29). That's why Paul speaks of having been "granted" the chance to suffer for His sake (1:29).[26] All things become gifts in Christ, and all gifts are cause for thanksgiving to Christ.

Chapter 2

That purpose of preparing for suffering and affliction with thanksgiving is drawn directly from Christ's way of life. What does it mean that He came to serve and to give His life as a ransom for many? The same "mind" (2:3) that was in Him in His state of humiliation – the time from His conception to His resurrection when He did not fully use His divine majesty – should be in the church at this time before we are glorified forever with Him in the resurrection.

In His humiliation, He did not snatch at good things, even when they belonged to Him, such as His equality with the eternal Father in the Holy Trinity (2:6).[27] Instead, the eternal Son learned obedience even to the point of the public execution as an accused criminal on the cross, terrible as that is. Since He did that and did not avoid the suffering, humility, or blood, God has highly exalted Him and given Him a Name – a fame and glory, not just a set of syllables – above every other name. Without the cross, there would be no glory; without the death, there would be no resurrection. First, He had to bend His knees to the Father's will; one day, every knee shall bow to Him. First, He had to confess the goodness of the Father's plan for salvation; one day, every tongue shall confess that He is Lord to the Father's glory (2:11).

That obedience – Christ's active obedience to God's law and His passive obedience to God's just wrath – is the pattern for ours. The need to "work out your salvation with fear and trembling" is not because God's rescue is unsure but because the road to heaven is narrow and hard. The world and its children are "crooked and perverse" (2:15), and it is dark. Yet we must walk through this world, and we shine as lights in this world (2:15). Even now, there are some to help us on this way, as Timothy and Epaphroditus[28] were sent to and known by the Philippians as examples and helpers in Christ. We are not alone, but Christ's way of life is difficult. We walk together, and the crosses we bear come from the God Who is Himself at work even now in our midst (2:13).

Chapter 3

Positive duties always have negative duties paired with them. If you should do something, you must not do its opposite. Suppose you should pay careful attention to Christ's pattern of humility. In that case, you must pay no attention at all to any preacher or church who tells you that Christianity is the farthest thing from humility or affliction or trouble. Such were the "circumcision party" who followed Paul everywhere and

---

26 1·29 is part of a large catena in FC SD II·26 attesting the need for God to open our understanding and hear to understand the Scriptures.

27 2·6 is cited in FC Ep. VIII·16 concerning Christ's state of humiliation until after His resurrection.

28 To define "liturgy" and "liturgist," Melanchthon uses 2·25's description of Epaphroditus in Ap XXIV·82 to prove that "liturgist" does not mean one who makes a sacrifice.

troubled his churches greatly. Paul sternly warns the Philippians to pay no attention to people whose Christianity has no place for suffering or waiting for Christ's rescue. Such people put "confidence in the flesh" (3:3, 4), a trust in some human quality either of an individual or a group that does not trust in Christ and opposes trust in Christ.

By their own lights, Paul's opponents should admit that Paul has more reason for confidence in the flesh than anyone. They want everyone to be as Jewish as possible, and Paul asserts that he is a better Jew than anyone (3:5-7). Still, he calls all those qualifications and credentials so much "rubbish" or "loss," polite terms in v. 7 for what is really the grossest thing you can think of throwing out in the trash.[29] All of it is absolutely the grossest, stinkiest piece of trash compared to knowing Christ and being known by Him in the resurrection. So, Paul is happy to throw all those credentials in the trash and hold instead to Christ's promise. The end of "confidence in the flesh" is destruction, not resurrection to life. Evil men with minds set on evil things receive evil things in the end (compare Psalms 1 and 18).

Paul speaks in the first person throughout much of this chapter (3:4-18 in the singular, 19-21 in the plural) because he is clear on the stakes of trust in Christ. Christianity is no idle hobby. Doctrine is no passing interest. The resurrection is his life's goal and every Christian's goal, and it can only be obtained through putting aside confidence in the flesh and holding fast to Christ's words. In the pattern of His resurrection, we one day obtain a resurrection, too (1:17). His suffering, death, and resurrection are the pattern for our lives, and His power will accomplish all those things if we trust in Him (1:12).

Chapter 4

The pattern of joy and thanksgiving that the Philippians saw in Paul is the pattern of their life together even now, should they never see Paul again. People at odds should reconcile, and hardships at odds with our flesh should be received with joy because the Lord's coming, the Last Day, and our resurrection to everlasting life may come at any time. The New Testament does not teach that at some point in the past, everyone thought Jesus would come back soon. The New Testament teaches that all Christians should always think that Jesus will come back soon because He may. Our readiness and watchfulness are known chiefly through the manner of life we live – the pursuit of good things (4:8) and the rejection of anxiety and fear (4:6) because God's peace fills us now (4:7).

> *Sincerely, Paul finds his life's purpose in the resurrection. This is not "pie in the sky by and by" because it is not wishful thinking that someday things will be better. It is the athlete's firm conviction that what he suffers now is worth the prize he stands to win.*

This is not what the world usually calls "the good life" because our good life in Christ may have imprisonment, such as Paul's, or opposition, such as Paul's, or death in the near future, such as Paul's. A life such as Paul's is our pattern in Christ (4:9) because only a life with confidence solely in Christ has a good end. Only trust finds its way to resurrection. The flesh, what it imagines would be good for us, and the stupid confidence in it will all be disappointed. Setting our minds on things above, on the goal of the upward call of God in Christ Jesus' triumphant shout, we know where we are headed and find peace and joy already on the way there.

---

29 Works are injurious to one who trusts in them, FC SD IV·37, 3·7ff.

COLOSSIANS

AUTHOR

Paul writes from Rome (most likely) in his captivity (1:1).

COMPOSITION AND PURPOSE

Unlike the other captivity letters, such as Ephesians, 2 Timothy, or Philippians, which were written around the same time, this letter has a direct, difficult situation in its background, similar to the generally longer letters of Paul's time of free movement and ministry, such as Romans or the letters to the Corinthians. False teaching about the worship of angels had spread so widely in the church at Colossae that Paul had to correct what was amiss in their teaching and practice.

OUTLINE

1:1-12	GREETING, THANKSGIVING, AND INTERCESSION
1:13-2:7	THE IDENTITY OF CHRIST IN TRUTH
2:8-23	THE REALITY OF FALSEHOOD ABOUT CHRIST AND THE ANGELIC POWERS
3:1-17	THE OLD MAN AND THE NEW MAN IN CHRIST
3:18-4:6	THE CHRISTIAN HOUSEHOLD
4:7-18	COMMENDATIONS AND FAREWELLS

CONNECTIONS TO THE OLD AND NEW TESTAMENTS

Colossians does not have extensive quotations from the Old Testament, and there is debate about whether it has any direct quotations from the Old Testament. Instead, it relies on how the Old Testament distinguishes between the divine Messiah (see 1:20 to Isaiah 53:5, for example) and the false traditions of men (compare 2:22 to Isaiah 29:12). The false teachers Paul here opposes do not look similar to the same mixture of Jewish mythology and careful legal instructions he faces at many other points in his ministry. Colossians is thus the captivity letter that most resembles a letter such as Galatians or Titus from his time of freedom.

CHAPTER 1

The letter strongly resembles Philippians because the imprisoned apostle again writes to a congregation in need of understanding affliction and cross-bearing in Christ. However, it differs from Philippians in the depth of error at Colossae. Where the Philippians needed to connect Christ more definitely and clearly to this life's hardships, the Colossians had been drawn away from Christ toward worshipping angels (2:18).

The apostle thus begins after his customary thanksgiving with a strong confession of Who Christ is – the eternal image of the invisible God (1:15) – and what is His – all things and that in subjection to Him. His cross has made peace by canceling out sin's debt and accusation (1:20), and now Christ is working to present us blameless before Him on the Last Day. The entire cosmos has been put in subjection to the once-suffering, now-reigning Savior, things in heaven subject and things on earth subject.

Paul's apostleship has been to announce this to the nations, who in past ages did not know these things and thus worshipped falsely. Now, all must know the power and authority of the Christ so that all men may be completed through Christ (1:28). Without Christ, they do not find their full purpose nor their true end. Even in his suffering and affliction, Paul has done this because suffering and affliction remain for Christ's body on earth, the church. Such sufferings bring Paul joy because they are for that church (1:24) purchased with Christ's own blood.

CHAPTER 2

Against these realities, a strange delusion has come among the Colossians as also the Laodiceans nearby because some have brought "philosophy and empty deception" (2:8) to enslave them to the "elementary principles of the world," those angelic powers who became demonic in their fall. This connection between demons and "traditions of men" (2:8) must be explained clearly because we are unfamiliar with the angelic and demonic importance of following either God's Word or men's traditions. The angels obey only God's Word, and when men heed the Lord, they are like the angels in obeying only God's Word. The demons disobey God's Word, and when men listen to merely human teachings and not to God's Word, they are like the demons.

> The "traditions of men" are not simply wrong because tradition is wrong. Far from it! Tradition is not wrong on its own, but men's traditions quickly replace God's Word when they come into the church. The focus soon shifts from what God commands to what men demand. Angel worship accompanies men's traditions at Colossae because errors go swiftly from bad to worse to terrible. Paul's correction is a recalling of the Colossians to the firm ground of Scripture away from tradition's sinking sand.

Enslavement to the traditions of men is enslavement to demons who love to put contradictions and falsehoods on men's lips. In keeping the Colossians from the traditions of men, Paul would keep them also from the demons who require idolatry, blasphemy, and false worship (2:18), all of which have their own hallowed forms that do not free you from sin (2:23). Instead, he supplies them with the truth concerning the majesty and truth of Christ's identity (2:9).[30]

The Colossians have fallen prey to such false teaching and false teachers who have insisted that certain days or foods or times are holier than others, none of which has to do with the basics of Christian worship: the reality of baptism to make us alive with Christ (2:11-13) and abstaining from doing what we want and doing instead what God wants (2:23). Their worship expresses their false doctrine, which is unable to kill the body of sin or raise them to new life as God's true teaching and practice do (2:13).

---

30 2·9 is used in FC Ep VIII·37 proving Christ's possession of all knowledge, is equivalent to Jn. 1·14 and other passages showing that the two natures, unchanged, are personally united (FC SD VII·36), the divine and the human natures are personally united in Him (FC SD VIII·30), at FC SD VIII·70 to indicate the human nature's indwelling of the entire godhood according to the personal union.

They should abandon such false teaching and practice because it has no power to save, unlike the powerful body of Jesus that was nailed to the cross and thereby disarmed all His enemies (2:15-16).[31] He is the Ruler, and His Word should be heeded. All others must be silent.

Chapter 3

The focus of the Colossians' lives is, therefore, Christ's life because only He is able to defeat their enemies. Looking to the day of resurrection, they must put aside those practices that self-made religion has been unable to destroy in them: lust, greed, and other such defiling things that make their consciences afraid to meet the Lord on that great Day. God's wrath will surely come upon such disobedience (3:6), both gross and secret sins (see the list in 3:8).

Instead, right now, the church must speak in a new way with each other – in truth, not in lies or deceit (3:9) and hold fast to the new man each has become through his baptism, full of the Spirit's fruit (3:12). The transformation is not of everyone into a circumcised Jew as the false teachers taught (2:11). The transformation of each Christian is into the image of Christ (3:11) which is the image of God (1:15) full of love and mercy and truth. All this will take place and there can be no transformation without the Word of God (3:16). No Christians who are not in Christ's Word are transformed into Christ's image. Everyone must be changed, and every change must happen through the Word of God.

Those changes vary according to one's calling, so just as a general exhortation was followed by specific teaching about various callings in Ephesians 5, Paul follows the general teaching with very brief, clear application to various household members in 3:18-22, all of whom would have lived in the same home. Wherever one lives or whatever he does or is, he is like the slave admonished to "serve the Lord Christ" (3:24), not the "elementary principles of the world" that had enslaved him once.

Chapter 4

The fellow workers of various ethnicities in this chapter all join Paul in a common task, the very thing he asks of the Colossians. Whatever their station, calling, or ethnicity, the Colossians must pray and walk circumspectly toward outsiders and carefully handle their words (4:2-6). The apostle calls the church to understand itself as set apart from the world: certain responsibilities belong to other church members, and the whole church lives together as opposed to a world that has not yet been freed through Christ. To free that world, the Word of God must go forth even from Paul's prison cell, and he requests that the Colossians speed the Word along through prayers of thanksgiving (4:3) that will go where the enchained apostle cannot. Whatever he suffers or wherever he is imprisoned, Christ's Word nonetheless goes forth into all the world.

---

31   2·16 is copiously cited· at Ap. XXVIII·14 to deny the remission of sins to the law or human traditions, at FC SD X·13 to deny yielding to false apostles who teach adiaphora as necessary things; AC XXVI·25 (along with 2·20-21) to warn of the misunderstanding of traditions whereby men sought to merit grace; to prohibit traditions that merit grace along with all of 2·16-23 at AC XXVIII·44; in Paul's complaint about men seeking merit from the law (Ap. III·272); whether human traditions are necessary acts of worship for righteousness before God along with 2·17 (Ap. VII-VIII·35) and 2·20ff.

1 THESSALONIANS

AUTHOR

Paul writes at the instigation of a report from Timothy.

COMPOSITION AND PURPOSE

This early letter of the apostle dates from his time in Corinth. Since we know from an inscription that Gallio before whom Paul appeared (Acts 18:12-18) took office as proconsul in Corinth from midsummer 52, this letter would date from any time within Paul's eighteen months in Corinth, one of his most extended stays in one spot in his ministry. That puts our letter possibly in the year 50 or very easily sometime in the year 51 AD. He writes to the church he founded in Thessalonica to encourage them and to clarify for them the nature of the resurrection of all flesh and the end of all things.

OUTLINE

1:1-10	Greeting and thanksgiving
2:1-16	Paul's missionary work in Thessalonica
2:17-3:13	Paul's ongoing relationship to the Thessalonians
4:1-12	Purity, love, and honesty
4:13-5:11	The second coming of Christ
5:12-28	Life while staying awake and conclusion

CONNECTIONS TO THE OLD AND NEW TESTAMENTS

Since the Old Testament looks forward to the first advent of Christ, direct connections between the books of the old covenant and this letter are few to none. Instead, you will notice if you read Daniel 7-14 or the back half of the prophet Zechariah, their pictures of the end of all things are found again in 1 and 2 Thessalonians and the book of Revelation. Direct connections between this letter and the rest of the New Testament are found wherever the end is discussed: the final parables of Christ concerning the Last Day in the gospels, the discussion of the antichrist in 2 Thessalonians, and the depiction of tribulation and judgment in the Revelation to St. John.

Chapter 1

There are two advents in view through this letter and the second letter to the same church: the advent of Christ in glory with all His angels and the advent of the apostle among the Christians in Thessalonica. In the apostle's coming, they learned Christ and how to walk in

Him. In the Christ's coming, the worth of the apostle's teaching and instruction in these two letters will be proven. For Christ's second coming, the apostle still works diligently to prepare his children in the faith.

From the first, the Thessalonians have suffered (1:7) just as Paul and Jesus did before them (1:6) because the same truth brings the same crosses to all of us. Yet they forsook idolatry (1:9) and were converted to God in order to wait for His Son to return (1:10). The last things and the Last Day are not sidelights of Christian teaching. They are the focus of Christians' lives and Christians' hope, and in this letter and the one that follows it, these matters of the End become very clear through the Spirit's instruction in Paul's words.

Chapter 2

Paul first recounts how he brought the gospel to the Thessalonians and how he behaved among them, not asking them to support him but supporting himself (2:9). This care like a mother (2:7), and this teaching like a father (2:11), was to prepare the church in Thessalonica to walk in a way that glorified God. The Thessalonians heard and accepted Paul's preaching of Christ and accepted Paul himself. For that acceptance, they were persecuted by their own countrymen in Macedonia as the Jewish Christians in Judea had been persecuted by their own countrymen, the Jews. This persecution from one's own people-group is a great hardship since you least expect hostility from those closest to you. A foreign army could be expected to despise you. You do not expect your neighbors to want to harm you.

Paul's assertion that his countrymen, the Jews, oppose Christ and the apostles and indeed all mankind is part of his thinking about the mission to his own people. Look at Romans 9-11 and the commentary above for his prayers on his people's behalf. Here, we find his statement about the depth of their hostility to Christ and His church, for which he makes no promise that it will abate with time. His prayer in Romans is the other side of the coin to 2:14-16: a people so firmly opposed to Christ now would redound enormously to God's glory when converted, as the persecutor Saul glorifies Christ marvelously in his conversion and use as the apostle known as Paul.

Chapter 3

As in so many places, Timothy was sent by Paul to relieve the sufferings and isolation of the Thessalonians, whom Paul had been unable to see himself (2:18). Timothy's report back to Saul was uniformly positive (3:6), especially about the love the Thessalonians bear one another.

Of all the end-times topics by which many are fascinated, "love" is scarcely ever a subject-header among them. That's a measure of our biblical ignorance rather than of love's irrelevance to the end times. Whenever the prospect of the end is brought up, so is love. The love of some grows cold in the end, but the church is encouraged to love all the more fervently. For Christians, the possibility of Christ's return at any time (see 5:2) means the necessity of love at all times.

The visit of Timothy is evidence of Paul's love for the church, and the apostle's prayer is that God would cause love to "increase and abound" (3:12) in the church now. Why? Just as Christians do not fear Christ's coming, they grow all the more in love as their sense of His coming is sharpened. The strengthened heart (3:13) is the one growing in love to the very end, as Christ's heart found its goal in the death on the cross. If we have nothing to fear from His coming, we have everything to look for and hope for from His coming, and there is more reason for love abounding as we see that Day approaching.

Chapter 4

This frequently misused chapter[32] has been squashed into preset ideas about how Jesus must come back secretly at the time of something called a "rapture" from the Latin word for being "caught up" in 4:17. There is no rapture timeline or mention of a period of tribulation in this chapter, nor any of the other confusions and complexities men have concocted to say what Scripture does not say.

Instead, the picture here is obvious: on an unknown day that could be like any other day (5:3), Jesus will return openly, loudly, and visibly to His creation (4:16). Some saints will have already died before that Day (4:14-15). They will rise at Christ's call (4:16). Some believers will still be alive when Christ returns (4:17) and brought to the place of Christ's judgment pictured in Matthew 25 or Revelation 20, along with all others who have ever lived. This chapter focuses on the comfort for believers of that Day, which gives them everything to gain and nothing to fear. Christ comes once and then comes the Judgment and then the everlasting life. It is that simple, even if men prefer complexity.

> The "rapture," a secret snatching up of all believers in a secret return of Christ, has no place in Christian minds because it has no place in the Scriptures. The snatching up Paul describes is the fate of believers who are still alive at Jesus' return so that they are with Christ and their fellow believers at His coming. None of that will be secret since His return is announced by triumphant battle trumpets and all His angels. Nothing about His second Coming will be unknown or unsure.

It is simple because Paul's simple instructions about leading a life that allows you to have something to share with others (4:11-12) may strike many as unambitious. His goal is to have Christians ready, watching for Christ's coming, and doing the simple things Christ commands for His people before His coming. Blessed is the servant whom his Master finds busy! Cursed is the servant whom his Master finds idle and speculating about this day or that hour, matters no servant is given to know (5:1). Blessed rather are the hands busy with sharing his goods and abstaining from the world's deceptions (4:3-7) because that one imitates the apostle and is ready for the coming of the Master.

Chapter 5

As in the gospels, the Master's advent is cause for watchful readiness (5:6, 8). Staying awake means putting on the faith, love, and hope that mark Christ's soldiers (Eph. 6 and here v. 8). They fight against spiritual enemies whose end is destruction (5:3) because the End of all things also means an end to evil. Men may deceive themselves and others with messages of peace and safety when no one shall be hidden from God's judgment (5:3), but lies will be proven to be lies when the Truth Himself comes again in glory.

The chapter's admonitions to pray and pay attention to God's Word (5:19-20), to growth in discernment and avoidance of evils, and the imitation of the apostle and the love of the ministers (5:12-13) are all aimed at increasing love. They are the fruit of the increased love of God and the love of the brothers. They do not come about because the church is speculating about what day the world may end or what one of the brothers has done wrong, or how Paul should have done

---

32 The sole citation from this letter in the entire Confessions is 4.4 in Ap. XXIII·43 to prove Paul's command to possess his vessel in honor also in marriage XXIII·65. On that basis, we were not confessionally entirely prepared for the prominence of 1 Thess. 4 in aberrant end-times teaching in the last 200 years.

something differently. Such love is born out of knowing that the Lord is at hand and comforting each other with His nearness, coming kingdom, and blameless goodness. God has appointed us for salvation through Him (5:9), so how can we not walk in love, praying for the brothers and greeting them with the warmth of the Spirit?

2 THESSALONIANS

AUTHOR

Paul writes again with his coworkers Silvanus and Timothy to a confused congregation (1:1).

COMPOSITION AND PURPOSE

The first letter did not clarify everything. A second letter was needed to lay out more definitely what the end of all things would be and especially how power in the church would be misused to hasten the end, as Judas had betrayed Christ as the end of His ministry on earth. This letter shares with the first the same congregation a need to set things straight and steady fainting hearts. It gives certainty where uncertainty had prevailed.

OUTLINE

1:1-4	Greeting and thanksgiving
1:5-10	Divine judgment
1:11-12	Prayer for the Thessalonians
2:1-12	Christ's second Coming and the nature of the End
2:13-17	Thanksgiving doubled
3:1-18	Admonition and conclusion

CONNECTIONS TO THE OLD AND NEW TESTAMENTS

The creative power of the Lord's mouth (Psalm 33:6) becomes the instrument of His destruction of the man of lawlessness (2:8), just as the prophet predicted (Isaiah 11:4). The destiny of the wicked away from the eternal presence of the Lord (1:9) was the destiny of Cain (Genesis 4:16) and Jonah's attempted escape from the Lord's Word (Jonah 1:3). Connections to the Old Testament are many in this letter of final things if one has eyes to see, but they rely on the reader's knowledge of Scripture to make those connections, as does the complex, wondrous Revelation to St. John. Similar connections to the apocalypses in the gospels and to the first letter to the Thessalonians are more obvious.

Chapter 1

Why another letter on nearly the same subjects? In Satan's attacks on the Thessalonian church, he deluded some into believing that they need not work because Jesus would soon return (3:6). Letters and teaching are always necessary because we are weak and sinful and fall prey to delusions and lies. There would likely be no need for the New Testament letters if men were not so sinful. They might have preserved the apostles' teaching purely without needing letters. The traditions to which Paul refers (2:15, 3:6) could be many things, but the only things we know for sure Paul taught are what his letters contain. We dare not go beyond these letters and the rest of the Scriptures because we do not know how much could be corrupted in time if even the apostle's own words were corrupted in a congregation he himself had planted. We hold to the Scriptures as God's truth as we hold to nothing else in heaven or on earth because only in the Scriptures can we be sure that we are holding to Christ's truth, not Satan's lies.

Christ is clear that wicked men will suffer an eternal fire in hell with Satan and his demons, whether those wicked men have personally afflicted God's church (1:7-9) or not. The believer does not receive the damnation he deserves because he is justified by faith. The unbeliever receives the damnation he deserves because he has not trusted in the returning King. Continued rebellion against the King will be recompensed with the King's justice. And It will indeed be just, not too much, not too little, but a just return for the high crime of treason against the only Master.

Chapter 2

That treason has an architect, Satan, and among men, an assistant to the architect, here called the "man of lawlessness." Since "sin is lawlessness," this man is also called the "Antichrist" who sets himself up in Christ's place for worship, a chieftain for mankind's general rebellion against the Lord (2:3). That is why his revelation (2:3) is connected to a general apostasy where mankind exalts the Antichrist (2:4) rather than the Christ. These are not obscure matters of speculation any more than hell or the Second Coming of Christ are obscure matters of speculation. Indeed, this is so plain that Paul had taught it all before to the Thessalonians (2:5).

> This topic is copiously discussed in the Lutheran Confessions (Tr. 39, Ap. VII-VIII:4, SA II.IV.10-11) because the growth of power in the Roman papacy was the cause of the persecution and death of evangelical Christians in and after the Reformation of the church in the sixteenth century. Although the Scriptures also discuss "antichrists" in the plural (1 John 2:18), the office of the papacy is the antichrist (1 John 2:22, 4:3; 2 John 7) because it is the display of that man of lawlessness who opposes Christ's teaching and yet claims to speak for Christ with absolute authority and with absolute obedience due him.

The restraint exercised on that man (2:6) was taken out of the way when the Roman papacy (there are other so-called popes in other churches as there are other bishops in churches other than Rome) set itself in God's place, denouncing the gospel the Scriptures proclaim and replacing it with another way of salvation. In Paul's time, these things were not yet manifest, but over time, the claims of authority for the bishop of Rome and for his jurisdiction over all souls grew and grew. By the time of the Reformation of Christ's church, the pope had exalted himself to speak for Christ where Christ had not spoken and to deny the simple things of the Scriptures wherein Christ's Spirit is speaking still. The evils of the Roman papacy have only multiplied over history so that in our time, the popes have approved of an idea of salvation through other religions, salvation apart from Christ Jesus. Salvation through

Islam or Judaism or Satanism is proof positive of how the Antichrist is the chieftain of the whole tribe of unbelief. He leads the "apostasy" (2:3) because he leads Christians, in particular, into deception, comforting pagans in their paganism and teaching Christians that Christ was not necessary for anyone's salvation.

Such deception may be accompanied with "power and signs and false wonders" (2:9) as Satan's works often are. We should not be deceived by what we see, but we should hold rather all the more firmly to what we have heard from the apostolic teaching. We hear and believe what the Thessalonians heard and saw firsthand in Paul from the apostolic Scriptures of the New Testament and the prophetic Scriptures of the Old Testament. In them, we have plenty to give us comfort and hope and strength in dark and apostate times (2:16-17).

Chapter 3

If deceptive teaching is the root of apostasy, false living is the fruit of apostasy. Many who had already been deceived in Paul's time left off working, contrary to the apostle's clear example and teaching, as we saw in the last letter to this congregation. Since they have such an example in Paul, he refers them back to that example of work on others' behalf (3:7-9) for imitation. If people still refuse to work after this reminder, they must be given the cold shoulder for their own good so that they are struck to the heart, ashamed of their behavior, and amend their lives (3:14-15).

Is this contrary to the love that should abound and increase all the more among the Thessalonians (1:3)? Are the commands Paul clearly issues (3:4, 12) the opposite of the gentleness he should have when trying to love the unruly or difficult? By no means! Instead, Paul is stern with children who need correction and very gentle with children who need comfort. He is a master of distinguishing what each child needs to eat: the law's sternness in admonition to the stubborn man or the gospel's sweetness to the taste of a hungry man. The distinction of law and gospel explains the distinction of tones in various situations, the nature of what is commanded or exhorted or encouraged or proclaimed in multiple places, and the way that the apostle uses many tones, many moods, and many situations to present the one gospel of Christ that will sanctify the one church of Christ in the one truth for one goal of glory at His imminent return with all His angels.

1 TIMOTHY

AUTHOR

Paul writes to his beloved child in the faith, Timothy (1:1-2).

COMPOSITION AND PURPOSE

It is difficult to assign a date to this letter as it is to the letter to Titus because either could have been written at almost any time in Paul's ministry. The need to identify and appoint new leaders for new churches could arise anywhere. This and Titus seem to predate 2 Timothy because they give no signs of Paul's captivity. Still, both are concerned with extending the apostle's work through his disciple's preaching and organizing the churches in new places where the apostle has not reached himself.

OUTLINE

1:1-2	Greeting
1:3-20	Timothy's relationship to the apostle
2:1-4:16	Life and order in the church
5:1-25	Discipline within vocation
6:1-19	Instructions for various conditions of life
6:20-21	Conclusion

CONNECTIONS TO THE OLD AND NEW TESTAMENTS

Quotation of the Old Testament is limited to the law's admonitions about feeding men and beasts who labor to support the contention that ministers should be paid for their work (5:18). The instructions about various conditions accept the patterns visible in the Old Testament for life at certain ages, the roles of the sexes, and the qualification of ministers of God. Its nearest parallel in the New Testament is the very similar vademecum of Titus, meant for use in an expanding church organizing fresh congregations.

Chapter 1

This handbook for church life was intended for Paul's closest disciple, Timothy, to use as the church grew through preaching the Savior's gospel. Throughout this handbook – a book meant to be taken along in the hand like a travel guide – teaching and life go together. Ungodly ways of life are against sound or healthy teaching (1:10), and myths and speculations (1:4) do not promote the stewardship (1 Corinthians 4) of God's gifts that Timothy should exercise in his preaching.

Paul is a model or pattern of God's grace and for Timothy's ministry. God's grace is especially evident in the conversion of Paul because in his ignorant unbelief (1:13) he was a persecutor of the church and a blasphemer of God. Convinced of his righteousness according to the law, he was himself lawless, not using God's law the way it was meant to be used to expose sin (1:8). God displayed His perfect patience with sinners in bringing Paul to a true knowledge of the true God and of the divine Scriptures so that Paul might preach toward love, a good conscience, and sincere faith for all nations (1:5).

That preaching is a pattern for Timothy's ministry and thus for all ministers. Its negative side is the tearing down of all falsehood and all fruitless chattering in which preachers indulged then and still indulge too often. The "genealogies" promoted by Paul's predominantly Jewish opponents (see Titus 1:14) are "endless" (1:4) because lies can always go on. They do not have the clarity God's Word does. They rattle and blather and puff and blow, saying nothing and enslaving all. Their promoters and preachers do not even understand the words they use (1:7). Instead, Timothy must devote himself to the sound, clear words he has learned (1:19), not turning aside to evils like the excommunicated preachers Hymenaeus and Alexander, whom Paul had treated like the man in 1 Corinthians 5, in delivering them to Satan until their errors were amended (1:20).

Chapter 2

The instructions for prayer are instructions especially to men, who should pray with hands uplifted to God (2:8) rather than hands lifted in anger against one another as Cain raised his hand against Abel and slew him (Genesis 4:1-16). Those men should intercede in their prayers for all men because they are praying to the one Mediator between God and men, the only One able to hear and to act and to save (2:3). Therefore, they may pray even for heathen rulers (2:2), here called generically "kings," a title the Roman emperor would not use for himself but a biblical title for men in authority in any nation, because the only true God also rules over those nations that do not acknowledge Him and those kings who do not bow before Him (compare Psalm 2).

If the men must forsake anger and self-seeking vengeance, the women must forsake an obsession with outward appearances for things more valuable. Braided hair, gold, and pearls, and nice clothing (2:9) are not evil, but they are far less beautiful than good works, quiet learning, and a life ordered according to God's Word (2:10-11). Women must pursue true beauty and not imitate the ugliness of Eve's trespass. Instead, their usual pattern of life will be marriage and childbearing, two things that God has brought together (Genesis 1, Psalm 127, Psalm 128), so that they are saved through childbearing as their appointed way of life. "Saved" here does not mean they are saved because they bear children. No one is saved through good works according to his vocation. "Saved" means that trusting in Christ, a woman's life of good works is shaped especially by bearing children and caring for her family (see also Titus 2:3-8), as the man's life of good works is shaped especially here by the giving up of rage against authorities and against one another for a life of prayer and intercession to the King of Kings.

Chapter 3

The life of good works suitable for an overseer or minister of Christ is a life like Christ's. Like Christ, he is a one-woman man (the literal sense of 3:2), neither divorced nor polygamous, and most of the qualities necessary for him to have are personal ones, not academic qualifications. His aptitude to teach as the Savior Himself taught clearly and well (look at Matthew 5-7) is one qualification among many. A good teacher without humility is of far less value to the Savior's work than a decent teacher with great humility and love. A drunkard (3:3) or quarrelsome man with a ready tongue and wit may positively tear down God's church through his evils, however wonderful his words may be. As in the test the Savior provides of a tree and its fruit (Luke 6:43-45), the teacher or overseer or pastor (all equivalent words) is known through both his words and his life. Teaching and life always go together.

The deacon, another word in Greek for a "servant," seems a lower grade of minister than the overseer of 3:1. The deacon's qualifications are not much distinguished from the overseer's, and the church has historically made the diaconate a step toward the office of the ministry. The deacon is tested in his entrance into the office (3:10) and may advance further upon faithful execution of his duties (3:13). Here, there are deacons, as in Acts 6, who seem to be in or advancing toward the same ministry the overseers or bishops (alternate translations of the same Greek word) have. Overseers and deacons must maintain the same confession of faith or creed concerning Christ's passage into this world and up to the Father's right hand (3:16), which is a capsule version of the 2nd Article of the creeds as we know them.

Many wish that there would be some clearer order in the Scriptures for the church. Many Christian churches today claim a definite order in the Bible or in the church's history such as the Roman pope, a set of properly ordered bishops, a government by teaching and ruling elders, or any number of allegedly important governance structures. The Scriptures themselves provide a variety of terms for what are the same roles so that bishops may be called "overseers" or "elders," and deacons could be called "servants," too. The terms and the structure are not nearly so crucial as church bylaws seem to make them. Instead, the Holy Spirit puts forth two other things than structure as far more important: 1) the content of the minister's proclamation and 2) the content of the minister's character. If he attends to his teaching and life, his title will be far less important. Ministers were set apart or ordained for the purpose of propagating sound doctrine and living a sound life because Paul refers several times to the importance of Timothy's ordination (1:18 and 4:14 here, as well as 2 Timothy 1:6). Still, that ordination set Timothy apart not for specific job titles but for proclamation and a life ordered according to that preaching.

Chapter 4

No minister should be surprised by unbelief because the Spirit "expressly says" (4:1)[33] everywhere in the Scriptures that mankind is sinful and addicted to the lies sin

---

[33] "Did the Holy Spirit vainly forewarn of these things?" AC XXVIII.49 asks on the basis of 4.1. The

feeds upon. The form that took in Timothy's time, as it may also in ours, concerned the forbidding of marriage and the promotion of special diets that had a form of holiness about them without the power of godliness. Abstinence from marriage and food seemed godly, but one could not receive God's gifts of marriage or food with thanksgiving (1:5), as a Christian receives all things the Father gives. Paul uses the test of the practical effects in the life of the teaching of "liars" (4:2) to demonstrate the nature of their lies. Nothing is idle debate about difficult topics. The nature of truth and the nature of falsehood are readily seen in the lives of their promoters.

So, Timothy must have a different life than his opponents, not addicted to the myths that they are (4:7). Not even his youthfulness, a disqualifier for wisdom in the eyes of many, should deter him from pursuing the teaching (4:13) and the life (4:12) that are healthy or sound in Christ Jesus. Perseverance in the Scriptures and in teaching them will be the salvation of the preacher and of the hearers (4:16). No divorce can be made between how the preacher lives, which should prove a model to his hearers (4:12), and how the preacher preaches, which is the focus of all his work (4:13).

> There are ancient sayings in the church to the effect that the minister's life is the people's Bible. This means that all God's people know of Him is what they see in the minister. This may have applied in other times when the people were largely or entirely illiterate. It is not biblical to expect God's people only to know their minister and not their Bible. They are God's people and must know God's Word (1 Peter 2:9-10), not primarily the minister's people. He is a shepherd but not their Master, and they must know their Master's voice, whatever the shepherd's life may or may not be.

Chapter 5

The church is God's family, so Timothy's conduct toward the different sexes and ages of the members is patterned on the family. Without knowledge of how to behave in a family, Paul's instructions in 5:1-2 are hard to understand because life in the kingdom is patterned on life in the creation. As the birds of the air are models of God's provision, the conduct of a good son with his father is a model of Timothy's conduct toward erring older men (5:1).

There are two classes of people who present particular difficulties for Timothy's ministry. One is any woman who has no man to care for her, and many of those women became wards of the church (5:9). Paul is very clear that if a woman has family to care for her (5:4, 8) or may marry again and form another family (5:11), she should be cared for by her family, and that anyone who has family in need of care – here and most likely in the ancient world, older women without an income or perhaps even a home to call their own – must care for his own (5:4, 16). The church will care for those who have absolutely no one to help (5:9-10) and who is willing to help with the church's work (5:10). The church cannot supplant the family in caring for people whom God has put

---

last times are marked out by the promotion of such doctrines of demons forbidding the institution of marriage.

in their families to be loved there. The church has the family for its pattern (5:1-2); the family does not have the church for its pattern.

The second troublesome class is the elders or ministers, but their trouble does not lie in themselves. It lies in the church's reluctance to provide them a living for preaching the gospel (5:17-18), a perennial difficulty in the churches (see 1 Corinthians 9:9). Into the bargain, people are always very ready to believe any ill report of someone in authority, and when Paul admonishes Timothy to accept testimony against an elder only on the evidence of two or three witnesses, he is holding the church to a simple biblical minimum of evidence (Matthew 18:16) that applies to anyone.

He must remind the church here to follow that basic standard because evil men are eager to defame authorities in the church at the drop of a hat since Satan hates all authority anywhere. If the accusations are true, Timothy must depose the elder from his office since the ministry is not a right of any man but a privilege and a heavy responsibility to any who hold office in the church. This deposition must be public so that others may learn and profit from the fear of God such deposition should place in their hearts (5:20), the very reason that no one should be ordained quickly (5:22). It is possible that some in the office or out of the ministry may be hiding their sins from other men right now (5:24), but in the judgment all will become clear (5:25).

Chapter 6

The admonition to slaves (6:1-2) concludes the vocationally specific instructions the apostle gives in this letter, which agree with his instructions to slaves and masters elsewhere (Ephesians 6:5-8), and all such instructions provide specific examples of how to conduct one's calling in the fear of God rather than the fear of men that leads to hypocrisy and dishonest conduct. Instead, all Christians in any calling will both agree with Timothy's sound teaching and live sound lives according to it because opposition to sound teaching will be evident in its ability to debate endlessly and destroy the church (6:4-5).

Godliness or "piety," another good translation for the Greek word, is known in what one believes and how one lives. Ungodly men are not content because they do not see we cannot take anything out of this world (6:7). Instead, they love money, and the problem is their love, not the money. Money may be useful for getting the food and clothing with which a godly man is content (6:8), but the love of money is never satisfied and devours those who profess it, killed by their tragic love (6:10).

Godliness is a pursuit of things that do not fade away (6:11) and combat that wields God's Word until the battle is over (6:12). Even the rich man may be saved if he understands his true place (6:17) under God's command because he may forsake the love of money for the love of good works, a treasure of which he will not need to be ashamed at the Last Day (6:18-19). Timothy's life and the life of his hearers will be focused solely on the confession of Christ (6:12) and the life Christ has laid up for His beloved, the prize to which we all now press forward (6:14-15).

2 TIMOTHY

AUTHOR

The apostle writes from captivity again to Timothy (1:1-2).

COMPOSITION AND PURPOSE

With the other captivity letters, this one shares a date of the late 50s or early 60s, depending on one's guess at when exactly Paul entered the Roman incarceration system. The letter is a leave-taking on Paul's part and an example for Timothy of how to consider one's ministry and one's life in view of the resurrection Christ will bring to pass.

OUTLINE

1:1-5	Greeting and thanksgiving
1:6-14	Encouragement
1:15-18	Opponents
2:1-26	Directions to the faithful son
3:1-9	The last days
3:10-17	Exhortation to faithful conduct
4:1-22	Valediction forbidding mourning

CONNECTIONS TO THE OLD AND NEW TESTAMENTS

The apostle's life is a drink offering (4:6) like the fragrant offerings of Jacob (Genesis 35:14) and of Moses (Exodus 29:41). This beautiful description of a faithful life near its end is the most direct link to the Old Testament in this personal letter. It shares with the other captivity letters a clarity in looking back on life and on the life of one's disciples such as Timothy as well as a clarity about the end a faithful Christian expects to find from a kind and gentle Master.

Chapter 1

This companion to the first letter to Timothy is the private and human side of the first letter's public view of the ministry. Paul wrote of what should be among all the churches in the first letter to Timothy the beloved son. What should be among all the ministers and all the Christians in themselves, Paul writes of in this second letter to beloved Timothy. The life in Christ has these two sides: one corporate and public, one individual and personal. The individual and personal side is not unknown or "private" in the sense that there you may do or be anything you like, but it is one's own, not another's, in the way that Paul only is "poured out as a drink offering" (4:6), not Timothy now or any congregation. Each has his life in Christ together with all who are in Christ through faith, but each must live his life in Christ, not another's.

The promotion of that life in Christ continuing now in Timothy is Paul's aim, as it was the aim of Timothy's grandmother and mother before him (1:5) and as it has been the apostle's aim since Timothy's ordination into the ministry (1:6). In ordination, Timothy received God's Spirit to equip him with power and love and self-control (1:7), so that the young minister would not be discouraged or dismayed at the many obstacles to his work. Ordination is being set up to suffer for the gospel (1:8) because Christ appeared to abolish the powers that hold this old world together – death, above all – and to banish darkness and bring light (1:10).

For such a gospel of light and power against darkness and death, Paul was himself ordained or appointed and, therefore, must also suffer (1:12). There is no shame in such suffering because it accompanies the office of the ministry Christ ordained. Christ is so faithful that even the loss of life in this life is nothing since Paul has entrusted his resurrection life to Christ, Who is faithful in all things (1:12). We lose nothing at all in losing everything for Christ's sake. Timothy can and should hold to the standard of words and life based on those words that Paul taught him, a treasure entrusted to Timothy on earth (1:14) as our lives have been entrusted to Christ, Who will come again from heaven. In this life, some will reject the ministers of the gospel (1:15), and some will receive them and help them in their service (1:18), and in all things, Christ's judgment will be just so that the ministers need fear nothing besides the Lord of the Judgment Day.

Chapter 2

Timothy is not meant to minister alone. As Paul ordained him and entrusted him with the gospel, he should do likewise (2:2). In all his activity, he must focus on the office of the ministry, not messing around with other careers, as we would call them, or side jobs because soldiers focus on making war and farmers focus on raising crops. Christ's soldier must focus on Christ's war, and Christ's farmer must concentrate on his Lord's vineyard. Paul has worked at other jobs to supply what was lacking in support from new congregations, such as at Corinth and Thessalonica, but the way of Christ is that his ministers have a right to be supported by those to whom they preach the gospel. This way of focus is recommended to Timothy, and in that way of focus, Paul believes he will grow in wisdom about how to focus (2:7). In the Lord, we not only learn what to do, but Christ also supplies insight as to how to carry it out.

Timothy's focused labor for Christ, like Paul's, will be "for the sake of the elect" (2:10), all those who obtain saving faith through the preaching of the gospel and whom God has promised eternal salvation at last. The ground of our life of dying with Christ and enduring with Christ in our callings is that not even our denial of Him or our sometimes faithlessness can deter Him from being faithful to His good news promises. He cannot deny Himself and does not lie, and therefore we can trust in Him even in the worst sort of suffering (2:10).

The focus on Paul's instruction is always on Timothy's preaching and teaching, terms used to spell one another in many places (see 1:11, for example). Empty words and disputes that spiral into enraged confusion must be avoided, and Timothy must devote himself to understanding God's Word like a builder who builds well and has nothing to be ashamed of in his work (2:15). Lying preachers, such as the ones here claiming that the resurrection has already happened (2:18), are like a disease in the body, a gangrene that eats away at Christ's members. They may turn and become vessels of honor in Christ's house (2:21, see also Romans 9:23).[34] Timothy must focus on promoting the truth in his own life (2:22) and in the church's life (2:24-26), even in the gentleness with which he must correct falsehood. Many are lacking in knowledge (2:25), and the Lord's minister is there to supply what is lacking with the right measure of kindness, aptitude to teach, and patience with the difficult (2:24). That capacity to rebuke so as to gain the erring brother is part of the minister's art of giving the right portion at the right time to the right person.

Chapter 3

Proud spirits know nothing of this art. Arrogant men whose evils begin with their love of self (3:2) and end with the denial of God's power (3:5) should be avoided because a little leaven leavens the whole lump. A little obsession with the love of money (3:2) or a little malicious gossip (3:3) destroys anyone, as these proud boasters have already destroyed certain women they know (3:6) in their fruitless search for more of everything, unsatisfied as demons in their appetites for power, fame, and anything other people can give them. The difficult times Paul anticipates with such raving boasters abroad in the church are our times, too (3:1). There is no golden time in which all the ministers and preachers are godly, but in this last hour when Satan knows his time is short, many in the church will be so depraved that they are disqualified from the faith itself, much less from preaching it (3:8). This chapter is the inverse of 1 Timothy 3 or Titus 1, presenting a clear picture of the disqualification of ministers through pride, as if one turned the positive characteristics from the other two Pastoral Epistles inside-out.

Timothy knows how to conduct himself as a minister through the positive personal example of Paul (3:10). Imitation is the form of Christian discipleship where we learn how to be in Christ through someone or many disciples who walk that way before us (see 1 Corinthians 4 and 11:1). Timothy has found his example of suffering in Paul's suffering, but Paul's suffering is not unique. All in Christ will likewise suffer because Christ Himself suffered at the hands of a rebellious world (3:12), and false teachers will be abroad among God's people to deceive. A minister must focus on the Sacred Scriptures because they will enable him to do and to face and to suffer anything. They are his complete equipment (3:17) for teaching truth and correcting falsehood and for showing the way of Christ and correcting the erring brother so that he walks the narrow way straightly (3:16). The Scriptures are breathed out by the Holy Spirit so that through the ministers preaching in the church, God's people have everything they need for faith and for life. We need not fear deceivers or the many evils of the day because the Holy Spirit has everything in His Word that we shall need.

Chapter 4

Timothy's personal focus in his ministry must then be on preaching since through preaching God makes known His will and His ways in Christ Jesus to the whole world. There will be many

---

[34] "And St. Paul testifies in clear words that from vessels of dishonor vessels of honor may be made by God's power and working [citing 2·21]…For he who is to purge himself must first have been unclean, and hence a vessel of dishonor," FC SD XI.82.

moods in this preaching – some of it readily received ("in season"), some of it sounding odd for the times ("out of season"), some rebuking errors and errant brothers, some of it exhorting the church to faithfulness and steadfastness, all of it needing much teaching and much patience (4:2).

The times may be very unfavorable to such preaching. Men will not listen to these things because their sinful natures agree with evil and darkness and lies (4:3), especially to the myths such as Paul's opponents like to promote (4:4). This cannot deter the faithful soldier of Christ. He must endure the suffering the world brings him and evils within the church bring him and persevere in preaching the gospel, an evangelist's work (4:5). Paul himself is near the end of his warfare (4:7), but Timothy must take up the same arms and armor and carry it on to obtain the prize to which Paul eagerly looks forward (4:8).

The personal notes at the letter's end spell out in people's names and a brief remembrance of their deeds who has received Christ's ambassador and who has rejected him, who has received Christ in His preacher and who has rejected Him. At times, almost everyone stood apart from Paul, so his warfare was very lonely (4:16). This is no problem because the soldier of Christ is never alone. The Lord is always with him, standing fast with him and giving him strength (4:17) so that the Lord's will for his servant Paul as for all his servants shall always be done (4:18). Nothing can stop Him. In Him Paul and Timothy and we are all more than conquerors through such a One Who loves us and gave Himself like a good soldier up for us.

TITUS

AUTHOR

Paul writes (1:1) to his faithful child, Titus.

COMPOSITION AND PURPOSE

The same generality of purpose and occasion is found here as in the first letter to Timothy, but since it predates Paul's captivity, somewhere in the early or mid-50s AD would fit. Titus is charged with founding new churches and finding new overseers on the island of Crete and is provided with instructions for doing both tasks.

OUTLINE

1:1-4	GREETINGS
1:5-9	QUALIFICATIONS OF OVERSEERS
1:10-16	DESCRIPTION OF FALSE TEACHERS
2:1-10	BEHAVIOR OF CHRISTIANS
2:11-3:7	CHRISTIANS CONTRASTED WITH THE WORLD

3:8-11	ADMONITIONS TO GOOD WORKS
3:12-15	CONCLUSION

CONNECTIONS TO THE OLD AND NEW TESTAMENTS

The description of and prescription for various conditions of life in this letter make no sense without the deep sense the Old Testament gives of created order throughout life – in the family, in work, in all one's doings. The description of and prescription for the church make sense in connection with 1 Timothy and when one sees that order is necessary in the church (compare 1 Corinthians 12 and 14) as much as in any other realm of life.

CHAPTER 1

The faithful minister Titus received this letter to guide his work on the island of Crete so that he would abandon neither the apostolic teaching nor the apostolic life that goes hand-in-hand. Paul writes to him so that he would know how to plant and order churches rightly as the preaching of the gospel calls more and more of God's elect into His kingdom. For that elect Paul labors night and day, and his labor will continue through Titus' faithful use of the apostle's Spirit-wrought words.

That labor must have full-time laborers devoted to their task entirely (see 2 Timothy 2:4-7). The first test of whether a man should be an overseer is knowing how to manage his own household (1:5-6). Without such wisdom at home, how could he be wise in God's household of the church? Family life is not an arbitrary job qualification that no one meets. If Paul were joking, he would not immediately hereafter give examples of what disqualified men are like – rebellious, blathering, deceptive, teaching for dishonest gain.

The positive qualifications of 1:5-9 are as real as the negative, disqualifying characteristics of 1:10-13, and the requirements to avoid "Jewish myths" (1:14) such as Paul's opponents everywhere promote and that are upsetting many in Crete at that moment (1:11) are of a piece with what's said earlier in the chapter. All of it aims at preaching the truth, rebuking falsehood, and living according to truth instead of the sinful nature, which false teachers indulge in their preaching and in their own lives (1:12).

CHAPTER 2

"Sound teaching" (2:1) is always preaching toward people's lives because the right kind of tree bears the right kind of fruit. What is preached becomes what is life, so the preaching must be sound or healthy for life to be sound or healthy. A healthy life in Christ varies for different ages and the two sexes. Older men must be dignified in their ways, and older women must be there to help younger women nurture their own families well (2:4-5). The generations are not meant to be in conflict. They are intended by God the Holy Spirit here speaking to love one another and promote the good of the church's households (see 2:6, 9-10) because the gospel Paul and Titus proclaim is a gospel that has abolished ungodliness and worldliness (2:12) so that we may live a new life in Christ even in this present dark time (2:13).

Christ did not come to make us lawless. He came to buy us back, that is, to redeem us from lawlessness because sin is lawlessness. We are redeemed from sin's slavery to live in slavery to Christ, Whose service is perfect freedom. Titus' preaching and the preaching of the men he appoints throughout Crete will purify for Christ a people there in Crete for His own possession who are zealous for good works (2:14), as the preaching of God's Word does everywhere in every nation.

Chapter 3

Among those good works is the submission to authority and the calmness of tongue and spirit (3:2) that accords with accepting the Fourth Commandment in one's life. Unregenerate men are naturally enslaved to their pleasures and obsessed with destroying one another (3:3). On the other hand, God's kindness is known in Christ's appearing to abolish our hatred of authority and of one another through His grace in Holy Baptism. The beautiful description of the washing of regeneration and renewal by the Holy Spirit in Baptism (3:5-7) describes our change from the dark and miserable love of sin to the bright and glorious hope of life in Christ. We are not what we once were, and what we now are is all due to His grace, His washing, His purpose for eternal life.

Titus must speak confidently about these matters (3:8) because they are profitable for men to understand. As with Timothy, this Pastoral Epistle focuses on preaching, and even the prohibition of involvement with foolish words (3:9) is about what not to preach. Sound preaching is profitable (3:8), and unsound controversies and the preaching of them is unprofitable for God's people (3:9). A man obsessed with such unsound preaching, whether preacher or hearer, must be rebuked a couple of times before he is dismissed altogether for his love of division (3:10, and see also Matthew 18 and Romans 16:17). All of Paul and Titus' coworkers (listed in 3:12-13) help the apostle Paul and the minister Titus accomplish the one goal of the proclamation of truth that produces fruit among God's people. Without sound preaching, God's people would be unfruitful (3:14), but with His sound words constantly ringing in their ears, they are fruitful branches from the one fruitful Vine (John 15:5).

PHILEMON

AUTHOR

The prisoner Paul writes to his free brother, Philemon, on behalf of Onesimus the slave (1, 10).

COMPOSITION AND PURPOSE

In the time of his captivity (late 50s-early 60s AD) the apostle writes to his coworker in the gospel, Philemon, concerning the place and usefulness of Philemon's slave, Onesimus, who may be more valuable to the gospel work if returned to Paul rather than returned to Philemon, as Paul is doing according to civil law. The apostle writes to persuade his coworker that Onesimus would be more worthwhile in the gospel's service than in his own service (13).

OUTLINE

VV. 1-9	*Introduction*
VV. 10-21	*Pleading for Onesimus*
VV. 22-25	*Farewell*

CONNECTIONS TO THE OLD AND NEW TESTAMENTS

Like all other books of Scripture, this one does not overturn the existence of slavery, but it asks for a consideration of the slave above and beyond his economic status, the sort of brotherly care and love the law of Moses prescribed (see Exodus 21:2, Leviticus 25:39, 42, among others). Like the other books of the New Testament, this small letter evinces a change of status for anyone who is in Christ, changing the way we think of him and treat him because in Christ there is a new creation (11).

The letter is a masterwork of motivation in Christ. Paul asks for the former runaway slave Onesimus to be returned to the apostle, who had preached the gospel to him. Onesimus legally belongs to Philemon. Onesimus now spiritually belongs to Christ, so the apostle is pleading for Philemon to obey his own Master, Christ Jesus, to whom Paul, Philemon, and Onesimus all belong. Paul obeys Roman law in returning a runaway slave and asking Philemon to obey the law of Christ in treating Onesimus as he would Paul himself (17).

Nothing in this way of love and service can be compelled, and Paul does not want grudging acceptance from Philemon (14). He wants a free and cheerful heart to give the brother Onesimus an implicit freedom, receiving the runaway slave like an apostle of Christ, and maybe even a legal emancipation, even as Philemon owes his life to Paul (19). If there is any financial hardship, Paul himself will pay for it (18). It is a study in how to advise another Christian in making a good decision when that person must decide for himself. You can't make it for him. Paul cannot free Onesimus or bring him into any full-time service with Paul (as he had been doing, 10-11). Philemon can. Paul cannot ask the Romans to permit someone as lowly as Onesimus stay with him in prison and help him there (13). Philemon can. Paul is not taking away from Philemon's authority over Onesimus.[35] Philemon himself must give up such authority to command Onesimus to do whatever he wants, so Paul appeals to Philemon (21), knowing that love in Christ will show Philemon what to do.

For the apostle himself, in his imprisonment, is like the slave. He is not complaining about the injustice of his imprisonment or seeking to escape it. Yet he asks Philemon to pray that he may be freed from prison (22) and even be able to visit Philemon in his home, where the church meets (2), so that like human laws may not bind the slave Onesimus, the apostle Paul to one place but free to preach the gospel wherever it leads. Whatever men do or however they bind us, the Word of God is not bound, and it may change hearts to do things they never imagined before, as Onesimus was changed (10-11) and as Philemon might also be changed through the apostle's appeal.

HEBREWS

AUTHOR

Paul's authorship is disputed because the book is not structured like a regular letter until its end (13:22-25), when it sounds like Paul and names coworkers of Paul. Nonetheless, it is a fourteenth letter of Paul matching the other fourteen letters of the New Testament not written by Paul. Ancient manuscripts often list Paul as the author, and many placed this letter between Romans and 1 Corinthians among the other letters of Paul. It does not sound like a letter because it bears the marks of a sermon with the vagueness of reference (2:2, 4:6) that spoken words have, but written words do not have. It is the nearest thing outside the gospels to a sermon transcript, and it came into the New Testament on apostolic authority, as did all the other books, and the authority was Paul's. New Testament books are not written anonymously; this magnificent letter is no exception.

---

35 FC SD IV.17 uses v. 14 to explain "necessity" as sometimes indicating something wrung out against one's will, which is not how good works come forth from regenerate believers.

COMPOSITION AND PURPOSE

The letter addresses Jewish Christians, and that makes its purpose quite clear: that they do not turn again to the fruitless sacrifices of the temple and their former way of life in Judaism (Galatians 1:13). Rather, they must persevere in the confession of Christ despite the persecution that will come upon them and the feebleness of their own mortal frames. This rare fruit of the mission to the Jews was born from the need to keep people in the faith who had every reason to fall away and perish in the wilderness of sin like their fathers of old.

OUTLINE

1:1-2:18	CHRIST ABOVE OLD WAYS AND ALL ANGELS
3:1-19	CHRIST ABOVE MOSES
4:1-13	CHRIST ABOVE JOSHUA
4:14-7:28	CHRIST ABOVE THE AARONIC PRIESTHOOD
8:1-10:18	CHRIST'S WORK PERFECT, ALL OTHERS IMPERFECT
10:19-13:17	EXHORTATIONS TO PERSEVERE IN FAITH
13:18-25	CONCLUSION

CONNECTIONS TO THE OLD AND NEW TESTAMENTS

The connections to the Old Testament through quotation and allusion are too numerous to list, almost as many as Revelation's. Particularly important is the nature of the Melchizedek priesthood from Genesis and the Levitical or Aaronic priesthood from the law of Moses, the former for fulfillment in Christ and the latter by contrast with Christ's priesthood. What was imperfect in the service of the Old Testament tabernacle is perfected in the service of Christ in the heavenly tabernacle. Hebrews, therefore, gets to the heart of each gospel, all four of which revolve around the sacrifice of Christ our Great High Priest upon the cross. What is told in the gospels is explained in this letter. What is pictured there is lined out in its full significance in this chapter.

CHAPTER 1

A cascade of Scripture quotations follows a ringing introduction to this powerful sermon. The introduction pulls us into the sense that all time has led down to the point of Christ's coming. Now that He has come, we see the "radiance" of God's glory and the "exact image" or "express image" of His nature, so that in seeing the Son, we see the Father and know One far more powerful than the angels (1:4).

Since all time has led down to the time of His coming, all the Scriptures testify to His nature and might. From 1:5-13, this chain, or what is technically called by the Latin word catena of quotations, is brought together to attest to the divine nature of Jesus and to contrast that nature with the nature of the angels. Christ is not one among many and does not share a nature with the angels, whose nature is to serve mankind (1:7, 14). He is the unique and eternal Son of the Father (1:5, 6, 8-13) and shares a nature with us as true Man. The rest of the letter comes down like a waterfall from this great height, the merciful work of our Great High Priest proceeding forth from the glories of His two natures united in the One Person of the Son for our salvation.

Chapter 2

Why this sermon? Many are apt to wander away and stumble in the wilderness on their way to the land of promise. Many are apt to "neglect so great a salvation" (2:3), and the preacher, Paul, would have the hearers pay even closer attention than when they first believed. Now is not the time for straying and confusion because though the giving of the law came with great glory and people wandered away from it (2:2), how terrible is it if people neglect the glory of the gospel after having believed it (2:3-4)?

The law was given through angels (2:2), but the gospel came through the divine Man Christ Jesus (2:5-8). Therefore, the whole world is already subject to that Man, though we do not now see its subjection to Him. We await more from Him and His kingdom (2:8).[36] The angels were greater than He for a time (when He suffered), but now He has received a crown of glory and honor for His work of tasting death on behalf of all mankind that all mankind might taste life by His grace (2:9). His perfection had to be through His suffering (2:10).

His perfection was for our sake because He has become our Brother and is happy to be called so (2:12-13). He has shared with us in everything so that in sharing our death, He might share His life with us (2:14). None of this was for the benefit of angels but because He loves mankind (2:16). God's wrath has been taken away through His work of suffering. God is now pleased or propitiated (2:17) for the sake of Christ's suffering and death.

Chapter 3

> The contrast between Moses and Jesus and the covenants they brought to mankind appears prominently in John's gospel and Paul's letters. What the old covenant written on tables of stone could not accomplish, the new covenant written on the human heart with the blood of Christ does. Paul's opponents consistently misunderstand the old covenant as a way of life. It is only a way of death, and life is only found through the new covenant in Christ's blood.

But Christ not only surpasses the angels in His excellence. He also surpasses the chief figure of the old covenant, Moses, to whose law the Jerusalem temple was dedicated. Now begins the letter's or sermon's long proof that the ways of Christ surpass the ways of Moses and the mountain He speaks from is far better than Mount Sinai (see 12:18-24). This includes the discussions of the change of priesthood, the change of law, and the change of sacrifice between the

---

[36] The manner in which the two natures in Christ exist in the personal union with one another is made clear through 2-8 with a host of other quotes to the effect that "...to quicken, to have all judgment and all power in heaven and on earth, to have all things in His hands, to have all things in subjection beneath His feet, to cleanse from sin, etc., are not created gifts, but divine, infinite properties; and yet, according to the declaration of Scripture, these have been given and communicated to the man Christ..." FC SD VIII.55.

old and new covenants. Jesus and Moses were both faithful, but Moses was neither an "Apostle" nor a "High Priest" (3:1), and Moses was built, as it were, but Christ the Builder is greater by far (3:4). The status of 'servant of God' is a great honor, but the divine nature of Christ as the Son surpasses it (3:5-6). Thus, the direct address in quotation (3:7-11) and the admonition to tear out unbelieving hearts from the assembly (3:12) is urgent because although Moses led a people through the wilderness long ago, any moment now Christ may return. It is only "today," a day for repentance if He desires it. All life is lived in view of a day when day and night shall be no more. As long as day and night succeed one another, there is time to turn and not to be hardhearted, as were so many in Moses' day (3:16-18). The people of God in Moses' time are examples of unbelief (3:19), so we should not stumble and fall like they did on our way to our promised rest (4:9).

Chapter 4

The letter is addressed to a moving people, not one staying in place. There is more out ahead of the church than behind it, as long as the time has been since Christ's ascension and the going forth of the gospel to the nations. Therefore, the Sabbath of the law of Moses is a shadow of the rest to which we now press forward. They rested then for one day in seven, but we must persevere and not have evil hearts so that we obtain a rest of which the world has never seen the like. God's oath that the unbelieving should not enter His rest (4:3, 5) is an oath that nothing in this life, not even the rest and peace of Joshua's day (4:8), can provide what He has laid up for His people.

Disobedience cuts us off from that rest because it cuts us off from His voice. His voice, His Word, is not some idle sound but a mighty weapon to destroy our illusions and idols (4:12), piercing to our depths. Notice that the Word of God and the knowledge of God have come right next to each other, one after the other in 4:12 and 4:13, because in knowing God's Word, we come to know that He is all-knowing. If we stopped there, we would be justly and only terrified by the knowledge of God.

The rest we seek can, therefore, only be secured for us by One merciful and faithful with us, appointed by God as a High Priest to offer sacrifice for His people and make sure that they can dwell in God's presence. His human nature – the fact that He was tempted like us in every way yet without sin (4:15)[37] – is the assurance that He knows what faces us and yet is faithful to us so that we can come at last to the rest He leads us to, a rest Moses and Joshua have not yet seen but that our Savior has prepared for His people.

Chapter 5

The contrast with the high priest "taken from among men" (5:1) contrasts Jesus from the order of Melchizedek and all human priests under the law of Moses from the order of Aaron. They are like one another in needing to deal "gently with the ignorant and wayward" (5:2), but they are unlike each other in that each high priest from among men

---

[37] Essential to our salvation is the truth that Christ has assumed our nature, "however, without sin," citing 4.15 among others, in FC Ep. I.5-6.

dies and must be replaced. Jesus' death is instead the source of "eternal salvation" (5:9) for those who obey Him because He is of a different order.

The question whether this and the discussion that will follow for several chapters about the nature and work of Jesus' priesthood is too difficult to understand is one that Paul takes up directly before going on (5:11-14). His distinction here between milk and solid food is between immature hearers whose hearing is now dull (5:11) and mature hearers ready to understand how the Scriptures fit together with the apostolic witness to Jesus. That discernment is an understanding of the Holy Scriptures (5:5-6) meshing with the life, death, and resurrection of Christ (5:7-10) so that the mature Christian can distinguish well between good and evil (5:14). Discernment is at the same time "head knowledge" of the Bible and "heart knowledge" of what to do in life with that "head knowledge." The divorce between head and heart is not biblical. Head and heart work together in maturing to understand the Scriptures and what must be done.

Chapter 6

For the times are dangerous, and worse would be falling away from the witness of the Holy Spirit, whether the basics of the Christian faith listed in 6:1-2 or more difficult matters such as Melchizedek's priesthood, because to know the truth and then to cast the truth aside is very grievous. It is as if we would crucify Christ over again with the powers of this age (6:6) and display His shame before the world. Apostasy is an attempt at time travel. The apostate wants to go back in time to a time before Christ was glorified and back to a time before he knew Christ. He was a fruitful field and now bears thorns and thistles, the plants of the curse of sin. If he is bearing no fruit when the Master comes looking for fruit, his end is to be burned.

That general description of apostasy is not a statement that repentance is impossible. It is a playing out of the end of apostasy so that the hearers do not have a similar fate (6:9), as Paul explicitly says. His purpose is to make sure that the dulled hearing of his hearers (5:11) does not become finally and totally fruitless when the Master comes at harvest time. The Master's intention is that the hearers should receive the promises made to their forefather Abraham (6:13-15), whom they should imitate in his patience upon God's Word (6:12).

Our patience is not foolishness. It is the expectation that God will sooner or later deliver on His promises so that our hope in Him is called an "anchor" (6:19) because to hope in such a God Who promises and delivers is to drop anchor and be firmly fixed, though everything else changes. The ground of our hope is that One has already drawn near to God "within the veil" of the divine presence (6:19), and that One is our forerunner or pioneer, Jesus, Who has already gone where we shall go (6:20).

Chapter 7

If Abraham had faith and we should imitate his faith, Abraham also tithed to Melchizedek (7:4, 9), and Jesus' priesthood is like the priesthood of Melchizedek, appointed a priest and now living forever (7:3). The Holy Spirit says expressly that the descendant is in the loins of his forefather, his destiny wrapped up in his ancestors' lives. Thus, Levi, who would come generations later, honored Melchizedek through the honor Levi's great-grandfather Abraham showed Melchizedek. Scripture understands the generations as connected to one another instead of radically separate as we now imagine them to be, so Paul maintains that Levi already acknowledged the supremacy of Melchizedek in the tithe Abraham gave (7:9-11).

It is clear that Christ is not descended from the priesthood Levi founded (7:14), but His priesthood has only one other occupant – Melchizedek, the king of Salem. Psalm 110 announced that Christ would be in that priesthood. Since His priesthood differs from Levi's, the law also differs (7:12). The law of Levi's priesthood is that there are many priests because they are constantly dying and need another to take their places (7:23). However, Jesus' priesthood endures forever because He lives forever (7:24). The priests of Levi are weak and sinful themselves (7:27-28), but after the law of Moses, now there is a Priest Who is perfect and can thus offer perfection and fulfillment and eternal life to those whom He serves.

Chapter 8

That High Priest is our Christ, who carries on His priestly ministry in the heavens. Here, a difficult thing begins to be said: the earthly tabernacle and the temple in Jerusalem that came after it were merely "copies" of a heavenly tabernacle and place of God's gracious presence (see 8:2, 8:5, 9:11, 9:23). As the law is a shadow of the good things yet to come for God's people (10:1), the tabernacle and temple on earth, still standing when this letter was written (13:10), are shadows of the true tabernacle in the heavens into which only Christ our Priest has entered.

Therefore, only what Christ does can make us perfect since He deals with the reality, not the shadow. He is the mediator of a "better covenant" (8:6) because there would be no need for a second covenant if the first covenant, the covenant of Moses expressed in the law of Moses, had perfected mankind. Instead, the Scriptures themselves testify that a new covenant would come and abolish the old covenant that could not deal with sin and death, as Christ's covenant has abolished sin and death and brought life and immortality to light.

Chapter 9

The rehearsal of the basics of the old covenant and the service of its tabernacle (9:1-9) is to prove that what happens in the earthly tabernacle cannot cleanse the conscience (9:9) because it deals only with temporary regulations (9:10), not the eternal realities that Christ's new covenant handles. His appearance with His own blood in the heavenly temple means that a single sacrifice of one divine Man avails for forgiveness for all forever (9:15). This is why there is no need to repeat Christ's sacrifice and no sense in which it could be repeated, whether in the Divine Service or anywhere else. His sacrifice is done and was unique because there is no need for anything except His blood, even as in the covenant of Moses nothing could be accomplished without blood (9:18-22).

Christ did not work at the poor, small things of the Mosaic covenant that accomplished so little. He made one final sacrifice to do away with sin forever (9:26). Just as each mortal man dies and then is judged with no second chances or re-dos, Christ offered Himself once for all and will now reappear only to save those who eagerly await His coming (9:28).

Chapter 10

The law is repetitive because it cannot find what it is looking for: a perfect man performing all its statutes. Christ's covenant has no repetition because the sole source of holiness that all men need is available through the once-for-all sacrifice of Jesus (10:10).38 The priest may stand at an earthly temple as often as he likes (10:11), but the Christ sits enthroned forever at God's right hand with His reign always growing (10:13).

As the Scriptures long ago promised these things (10:15-18) and as Christ accomplished them (10:14), we can have confidence in our journey toward our Sabbath rest because Jesus has made a way for us to live and live forever (10:20). We can come near to God and know that our hearts are clean through His cleansing of our conscience (10:22), sprinkled with His blood as Moses once sprinkled the people of Israel with the blood of animals. What Moses' sprinkled blood could not cleanse – the conscience and the heart – Christ's blood is mighty enough to change and purify.

If we neglect to meet in Divine Service, we cannot know these things or encourage one another (10:23-25) and will, of course, not receive the benefits of Christ's sacrifice (10:26) because we have spurned them (10:27-28). The work of Christ is finished, but it does not benefit the man who refuses to believe it and tramples upon Christ and grieves the Holy Spirit of grace (10:29). God is not mocked by our indifference or blasphemy and will repay the one who deals faithlessly with Him (10:30).

The Hebrews had slipped from their former adherence to Christ when they were persecuted along with His people everywhere (10:32-33) and were kind to those imprisoned for His Name's sake (compare 10:34 to 13:3). Paul calls them back to their former confidence in Christ and to endure in the confession of His Name that they may receive His promise (10:37). The theme verse of Romans and Galatians from Habakkuk 2:4 reappears to remind the Hebrews that faith will be the hallmark of the man who finds everlasting life in Christ (10:38-39).

Chapter 11

The catalog of faith's assurance and conviction because of God's promise is a rundown of the Old Testament. Its characters are not defined by their virtues because some of them have many, such as Joseph, and some have very few when we see them in Scripture, such as Jacob the thief or Rahab the prostitute. They are not defined by their ethnicity as many of Paul's opponents defined themselves because some in this chapter were Jews, such as Isaac and Samson, and some Gentiles, such as Abraham before his

---

38 A single propitiatory sacrifice has been made for the sake of the whole world in the sacrifice of Christ, and no other sacrifice can be or should be made, per 10·10 at Ap. XXIV.22-23.

circumcision and Rahab. Some were wise, such as Moses, and some fairly foolish, such as Jephthah. What they have in common and what the people of God anywhere at any time have in common is faith.

Faith always has some outcome expressed in life: Sarah conceived (11:11), and Samson shut the lion's mouth (11:32-33), as did Daniel, who is not named here. Time would fail to tell of all the ways faith expressed itself in any given person's life (as time fails to make a complete list as Paul acknowledges in 11:32), but in anyone's life, faith is a conviction that God will deliver on what He has promised (11:6) and that He will be faithful to His Word.

Above all faith presses on toward something better than what now is because faith is unnecessary for any of us when we already have and see what we desire. Faith is only needed for someone who is traveling elsewhere with his life or in his life, pushing toward a better country than the one he now has (11:16). Faith is not at home in a sinful world, but it waits for the country and the rest God has prepared for those who love Him (11:16).

Chapter 12

All the faithful are a "cloud of witnesses" (12:1) around us encouraging us to find the same purpose and end they did, though they also faced sin and all sorts of obstacles on their own ways toward God's kingdom. More than that, Jesus is our chief example because He endured more than we (compare 12:2-3 to 12:4), but He lived and died as a Son and if God disciplines us through affliction and hardship, we will blessedly live and die as His sons, too (12:5-7). He would only fail to discipline someone who was not His (12:8-11). The temporary pain of discipline and hardship is nothing compared with the eternal pain Esau suffered when he traded temporary enjoyment for unending regret (12:16-17).

The sin that clings so closely (12:1) can spring up amid God's people (12:15-16), so we keep a close watch on ourselves. We do not come together (10:24-25) to enter a place where sinners are banished, and sentences of death are pronounced on all who fall short, as the sinners gathered around Sinai heard the sentence of death the law pronounced upon them and their livestock (12:20-21). The church's gathering in worship is Mount Zion, the heavenly Jerusalem (also called the "Jerusalem from above" in Galatians 4:26). The angels serve us here, and Jesus is here (12:24), and the blood we drink is the sprinkled blood of Jesus that does not accuse us like the blood of Abel accused Cain.

> *The Divine Service does not matter because of the number of people in attendance or the ornate vestments and art a church does or does not have. It matters because it is Mount Zion where Christ speaks and the blood sprinkled for our forgiveness is received. Churches that cannot or do not worship in reverence have not grasped the reality of Jesus' presence with His people so obvious in these final chapters of the letter to the Hebrews. As He was with the people in the wilderness, He is with us to the end of the age (Matthew 28:19-20).*

In this place of Christian worship, Jesus is speaking (12:25) even today, so His encouragement in divine Scripture to listen to Him while it is called "today" is an encouragement to persevere and endure with Him and not to turn back and be consumed in the wilderness (12:29). We want to see the city He has prepared, not the fire He has prepared.

Chapter 13

The commands and admonitions concerning the brothers (13:1), whether they are traveling (13:2), imprisoned (13:3), tempted to stray from their marriages (13:4), or tempted by greed (13:5) are all commands for the church to remain together, for the stones of God's holy temple to remain standing strong. Temptation will come to cut down the church's leaders because if Satan can topple the pillars, how will the house stand? So, leaders should be upheld in their speaking the Word of God (13:7) and keeping watch over souls (13:17).

Other voices are encouraging the Hebrews to return to the law and partake of sacrificed animals inside Jerusalem with other unbelieving Jews (13:9-11). They must not heed those voices telling them to turn back and to spurn Christ (see 6:4-8). They must instead go outside the city of the earthly Jerusalem (Galatians 4:25), where Christ went outside the camp of Israel to make atonement (13:12-13). They must be where He is and confess they long for the heavenly Jerusalem (13:14), not the one here on earth. Here, there is no lasting city, but since God has brought His Shepherd back from the dead (13:20), we will find the everlasting Jerusalem through His blood and mercy.

The General Epistles

The LETTER to JAMES

AUTHOR

The letter's author is the Lord's brother (Jn. 7:5, Gal. 2:12), not James the son of Alphaeus (Mark 15:40) nor James the son of Zebedee (Matt. 4:21). He is thus the bishop or overseer of the Jerusalem congregation prominent in Acts (see Acts 12:17 and 21:18 among others). Unlike Paul, he was not an apostle. Unlike Mark or Luke, he was not the scribe of an apostle. His connection to the risen Lord Jesus was direct and familial. He had seen his resurrected Brother (1 Cor. 15:7) and spoke of what he had seen and heard with the clarity and directness that Brother Himself had in all His teaching.

COMPOSITION AND PURPOSE

The church and her members are under pressure from the inside rather than the outside in this letter. Where Peter's readers suffer from the Gentiles, James' readers suffer their unique difficulties and sins. The letter may stem from a time after direct persecution when Christians already "scattered abroad" must hear from the bishop whom they once all knew and heard face-to-face and whose everyday work of guiding the faithful continues now in letter form. The letter shows how the faithful may withstand their trials and keep their faith through God's help.

CONNECTIONS TO THE OLD AND NEW TESTAMENTS

James' style is proverbial, a series of clear, brief statements set next to each other to form a line of thinking. He resembles Solomon in setting truths side-by-side to create a larger picture: Solomon showed the wise man and James the faithful man. James' brother, the Lord Jesus, does the same in the Sermon on the Mount. Compare these portions of James to his Brother's most famous sermon:

James 1:2 on trials with Matt. 5:10-12
James 1:4 on perfection with Matt. 5:48
James 1:5 on gifts with Matt. 7:7
James 1:20 on anger with Matt. 5:22
James 1:22 on hearing and doing God's Word with Matt. 7:24
James 2:10 on keeping the law with Matt. 5:19
James 2:13 on mercy with Matt. 5:7
James 3:18 on making peace with Matt. 5:9
James 4:4 on friendship and enmity with Matt. 6:24

James 4:10 on humility with Matt. 5:5
James 4:11-12 on judgment with Matt. 7:1-5
James 5:2 on riches spoiled with Matt. 6:19
James 5:10 on the example of a prophet with Matt. 5:12
James 5:12 on swearing oaths with Matt. 5:33-37

Other parallels with the teaching of Jesus, especially in the gospel of Matthew, are found in this letter:

James 1:6 on faith without doubting with Matt. 21:21
James 2:8 on love as the great commandment with Matt. 22:39
James 3:1 on teachers with Matt. 23:8-12
James 3:2 on the dangers of speech with Matt. 12:36-37
James 5:9 on the Judge at the door with Matt. 24:33

This letter's connections to the OT are thus especially rich in form, not in specific quotations or allusions, of which James has a few as well, mostly from the Law of Moses and a couple from the Prophets; Proverbs and Genesis are this letter's nearest relatives. In the NT, Jesus' speech patterns are audible in James' own love of diamond-bright, diamond-hard aphorisms (see the tables above).

OUTLINE

James' resemblance to Proverbs makes outlining the letter more difficult than one of Paul's or Peter's.

1:1-8		TRIALS AND THE WISDOM TO WITHSTAND THEM
1:9-18		WEALTH, TEMPTATION, AND THE GIFTS OF GOD
1:19-27		HEARERS AND DOERS OF GOD'S LAW
2:1-13		THE EVIL OF PARTIALITY
2:14-26		DEAD FAITH AND LIVING FAITH
3:1-18		QUALIFICATIONS FOR TEACHERS
	1-12	DISCIPLINE OF THE TONGUE
	13-18	REAL WISDOM
4:1-17		PARTICULAR DANGERS
	1-10	THE POWER OF THE PASSIONS
	11-12	EVIL WORDS
	13-17	VAIN CONFIDENCE
5:1-6		WARNINGS TO THE RICH
5:7-11		ENCOURAGEMENT FOR THE AFFLICTED
5:12-20		AGAINST RASH OATHS, FOR MIGHTY PRAYER, FOR THE SALVATION OF SINNERS

Chapter 1

Like Paul, James addresses the church as the Old Testament people of God. For Paul, the church is God's "Israel"; for James, the church of God is the "twelve tribes scattered abroad," possibly because of the persecution the church suffered in Jerusalem, where James was overseer. For all those people, his letter clearly describes faith under pressure. The man of faith is under trial from many sources and must withstand them all so that, like Jesus, he may be blessed under trial and not succumb to sin's deception.

The pressure comes from trials that cause doubt (2-8), the difficulties of poverty and wealth (9-11), temptation (12-15), man's wrath (20), and the deceptions of sin (21-27). Everyone undergoes trials that put his faith to the test, but if the test reveals a lack in the man, he cannot receive anything from the Lord when he asks with doubt that the Lord can provide for that.[1] The doubter is an unstable ship driven here and there by the waves with no fixed harbor. Like doubt, poverty and wealth can trick a man into believing that God despises him in his poverty or loves him in his wealth, though the gospel raises the poor man and brings down the rich man. James echoes Mary's song in describing the poor and the rich.

At the chapter's center is the nature of temptation and God's goodness. Without the clear understanding that temptation has its source in our inborn sin and its fruit in our desire to gratify sin, we may resort to blaming God for what is our fault. We may despair of His mercy without understanding that God gives richly and gladly to anyone who asks. Yet He is unlike the heavenly bodies He set in the sky: the sun, moon, and stars. They change with the days and seasons. He does not change, a never-setting sun and a constant star, and we have become the first fruits of His creation by the Word He has given us.[2] We are all that we are in Christ because He is goodness itself and gives openhandedly to any who ask.

> Trial and temptation are two different things because God and evil are distinct. God is never evil, and evil is never from God. Trial and temptation may seem the same to us at times: the same worries, the same pains, the same duration. Yet trials come from God to purify us, and temptations come from the devil, the world, and our sinful flesh to destroy us. James teaches us that our Father is always good and gracious, shining like a sun that never sets. We can turn to Him in any trial or temptation for help, and He will answer.

Man's wrath and naivete about how deceitful sin is are foolish because they neither accomplish what we seek – a change in our situation that only God could bring about – nor do they show us truly who we are since we love to pretend to be something we are not. If we would not be deceived, we must investigate His Word – the "perfect law of liberty" – to see ourselves honestly. James' test for being religious is what one does in visiting

---

1   1·6 used in LC Lord's Prayer – 7th Petition 123-124 to rebuke those who cannot say Amen from the heart because they "despise God and reproach Him with lying and therefore they receive nothing."

2   1·17 is used in FC SD II·26 to summarize the monergism of the gifts we have and at FC SD VIII·49 to define the divine nature as changeless, and 1·18 is explained in Ap. III·126-129 as not positing regeneration by works but as censuring "idle and secure minds."

widows and orphans; not what one says even to himself. The man who will withstand trial is the one who knows himself according to God's Word as owing everything to God and receiving everything for each day from God.

Chapter 2

This chapter does not contradict Paul's teaching because the Holy Spirit cannot lie or contradict Himself. Paul wrote of how a man is justified by faith. James wrote of how a justified man lives faithfully.[3] The justification and the faith are the same, and Paul and James are two sides of the same divinely minted coin. The pastoral problem of this letter is that men are trying to live without a living faith – such faith that naturally produces works – and yet claim to be Christ's. No one who trusts in Christ will be without the good works Christ has prepared for all who trust in Him (cf. Eph. 2:8-10).

This problem is front-and-center in how people are welcomed or not welcomed into the congregation's assembly for the Divine Service. When God's people gather, who is seated graciously, and who must find his way to a lesser place? Partiality (2:1, 4) is the preference of one man for another, even on the grounds of wealth or poverty, despite God's welcome to the poor and the haughty behavior of many wealthy men toward the church. The apostle adjures the church to welcome the poor as they do the rich because not to welcome the poor is not to love the neighbor. If we neglect the love of the neighbor, however humble he is, or filthy his clothes are, we neglect God's law and sit as judges over it that royal law rather than doers of that law. The man who does God's law sets himself up as a humble doer, not a judge, and therefore, he can expect mercy in the end from God, who is alone a judge of his law. The man who does not do God's law sets himself up as a judge and can expect only judgment because he has been arrogant and judged God Himself in judging which parts of God's kingly law he wants to do or ignore.

James' interest in justification springs from his interest in the practical behavior of the congregation. If someone should say that he is a Christian and has faith but neglects the poor, he is not justified by such dead faith. Let him look at his behavior to understand what sort of faith he has. Abraham and Rahab were "justified by works" because their faith in God's promise or God's power was expressed through their actions. If someone wants to neglect the poor or not offer up his son as a sacrifice when commanded or not welcome the spies Joshua sent, he may claim to have faith, but it is no faith Jesus would recognize. Such faith without works is "dead" (2:26), like a body without living breath. While Paul proclaims that only faith justifies, James proclaims what sort of faith justifies.[4]

---

[3] FC SD III·42-44 clarifies that James speaks concerning the works of the already justified, citing the Apology, and explaining that "if the question is, wherein and whereby a Christian can perceive and distinguish, either in himself or in others, a true living faith from a feigned and dead faith, (since many idle, secure Christians imagine for themselves a delusion in place of faith, while they nevertheless have no true faith.)"

[4] 2·21 explained in Ap. III·131-132 as James "commends only such works as faith produces." 2·24 taken up in Ap. III·123-125 as a discussion of "such works…as follow faith, and show that faith is not dead, but living and efficacious in the heart."

Chapter 3

The books mostly closely linked to James' letter outside the New Testament are Proverbs and Ecclesiastes, books of wisdom that describe life well and advise what to do among the confusions and changes life brings each of us. In Jesus' teaching, you will also find similar warnings about the tongue because of its power to destroy a church or a family that no other member of our body has. Therefore, the apostle's theme is the evils of the tongue and the nature of wisdom that would preserve and not destroy.

What James here calls "teachers" are elsewhere called "bishops" or "elders" in the New Testament and are now usually called "pastors" or "ministers." The teacher is in particular danger because his calling to preach is a calling of the tongue. The risks of setting things afire through false teaching and false admonition are heightened in his calling, though the risk of destruction through cursing, slander, and libel belongs to the whole human race. Every tongue is a firebrand-in-waiting if we do not bridle its power.

> *Of all our members, the tongue is the most destructive. That seems strange since the fists could kill, but tongues ruin more lives than fists do, though they do not often take lives. With the tongue, a good reputation is taken from an innocent man, and by the tongue, the closest relationships can be destroyed by words that cannot be taken back. Teachers or ministers are subject to severe scrutiny because their tongues speak for God, so the ordinary dangers everyone has from his own tongue are multiplied by the risks of misusing or defaming God's Name through false teaching and evil living.*

Bridling and control of the tongue and oneself are God's gifts. If one lacks those things, only let him ask God, who loves to give openhandedly. So that we know what we must ask, James lays out the difference between the divine wisdom God gives and earthly "wisdom" or cunning men devise. God's wisdom has characteristics of moderation, calm, peace, lack of pretense, and other things described here and exhibited in the Lord Jesus. Human "wisdom" is displayed in the opposite of the Lord Jesus' behavior: grasping, boasting, and demonic. The one who makes peace through his tongue does not set the world ablaze. That peacemaker, blessed as a son of God, instead sows peacefully a harvest that shall bear abundant fruit. His tongue leads to blessing for others as he uses it to bless. This vision of a wise life is the Lord Jesus' life lived out in His people's lives as they ask Him for everything needful for blessing.

Chapter 4

Why, then, is there any dissension among His people? Why are there war and envy among them? Because the faith they claim to have is not the faith of the Lord Jesus, a faith that dares to ask God for everything needful instead of snatching it from the brother. James does not specify whether all these problems are inside or outside the congregations because "friendship with the world" may exist inside a Christian church and a Christian's heart. It must be rooted out by asking God for what one needs instead of living in pride, which makes war on everyone and everything, including God Himself, if He gets in pride's way.

Pride draws away from God, judges the brother – who is only finally judged by God – and boasts about the control of time that is solely under God's power. Pride is the precise opposite of humility, and humility is the lion's share of repentance. The Pharisee in the temple boasted of himself even before God and thanked God that he was not like the people he judged. The publican was content to ask God for what he knew he needed. The humble man will always draw near to God, leave judgment to God, and ask God for the time he believes he needs for his affairs. There are finally only two ways of life: only sheep and goats, and only one way of life is blessed.

Chapter 5

What may seem scattershot here is held together by wisdom. Wisdom shows that riches are the source of great temptation and misery, outside and inside the church because it kindles greed, which holds wages back from a poor man most in need of a payday. The rich man favored among men may find great disfavor from the Lord should he forget that the poor are exalted through Christ and the rich are humbled through Christ, all to the glory of God who shows no partiality and gives liberally to all mankind.

The warnings given to confession, to prayer for great things such as Elijah prayed, to be reliable and not need the oath, to tell the truth, and similar practices such as one finds throughout the Sermon on the Mount have patience as their keystone. Impatience multiplies when we do not ask God for help. Patience grows through faith. James' entire letter is a letter of faith – what it is and, even more, how it is practiced. Faith has its own practices: humility, waiting upon God, prayer for all things small and great, love of the brothers,[5] wisdom in all its humility and peacefulness. The one with faith in Christ can withstand trials because faith receives strength, wisdom, and everything needed from the goodhearted, openhanded God Who has already given us all things in Christ Jesus. Having not spared His only Son, how can He not graciously give us all things?

---

5   5.16 is a proof of confession to the Christian brother, not to the priest, in Ap. VI.12.

The FIRST LETTER of PETER

AUTHOR

The writer is the apostle Simon Peter, also called Cephas. His knowledge of the Lord's teachings from the closest acquaintance during His earthly ministry and his preaching before both Jews and Gentiles are the cause of the letter's broad address to a wide swath of the church in many regions and the clarity with which he writes. This is the first of two canonical letters addressed to the great church by an apostle who traveled widely.

COMPOSITION AND PURPOSE

Since the church was persecuted in her Head and in her members from the first, this letter has no specific occasion for the suffering and persecution it addresses. The addressees are in various parts of Anatolia, the peninsula now entirely within the modern country of Turkey. The writer speaks from what he calls "Babylon" (5:13), a pseudonym for the city of Rome (Rev. 14:8). The apostle would persuade the Christians to endure suffering in the image of Christ and to live lives honorable and worthwhile in God's sight, whatever the world thinks of them or does to them.

CONNECTIONS TO THE OLD AND NEW TESTAMENTS

Peter's words significantly overlap with Jude's letter and Mark's gospel, likely due to Peter's close acquaintance with the Lord's brother and the second evangelist. His quotations from the Old Testament are frequently from the Psalms and the major prophets, including Isaiah. The letter's length means the apostle does not quote anything at length but uses the Old Testament as a source to begin his thinking about Christ and to finish his understanding of what the gospel means for our lives.

OUTLINE

1:1-2	GREETINGS	
1:3-2:10	OUR RESCUE FROM ALL PERILS AND FROM DEATH	
	1:3-9	THE BLESSINGS OF THE GOOD NEWS OF CHRIST
	1:10-12	THE HISTORY OF OUR SALVATION
	1:13-16	WHAT LIFE BEFITS THIS GREAT SALVATION
	1:17-21	THE GROUND OF OUR CONFIDENCE IN THIS SALVATION
	1:22-2:3	PRESENT DUTIES FOR FUTURE HEIRS

	2:4-10	The church's nature
2:11-3:12	Tables of duties	
	2:11-12	Duties in the world
	2:13-17	Duties in the state
	2:18-3:7	Duties in the home
	3:8-12	Duties in the church
3:13-4:19	Suffering and its ways	
	3:13-17	The blessing of Christian suffering
	3:18-22	Christ's example of suffering
	4:1-6	Suffering in this body of flesh
	4:7-11	Holiness in suffering
	4:12-19	Encouragement for sufferers
5:1-11	The church's holiness and the Christian's holiness	
5:12-14	Conclusion	

Chapter 1

Like James, Peter writes to Christians scattered abroad and undergoing trials and hardships. Is such suffering so strange that they should lament, or is it proof of their lives' anchor in Christ? Do they need to change their ways, or is constancy the key in times of upheaval? The fervent apostle who himself fell away at the Lord's trial but was restored through the Lord's grace writes of the demand for steadfast faith and the kindness of the Lord in words glowing with fire.[6]

Blazingly clear is the goal of the Christian life: the eternal inheritance prepared for them that nothing on earth can take from them. This "salvation of your souls" (1:9) is the object of their walk through the fire, those trials, afflictions, and difficulties they face for now, though that time will be short compared to the glory of life everlasting.[7] For all that, God is "blessed" (1:3) because He has prepared these things – all three Persons of the Holy Trinity working together for our salvation – and The powers of men cannot shake him. Christ is above all the powers, and we are sprinkled with His blood. Our inheritance is sure because of Him and His work for us.[8]

The Christian then looks to the day when all this becomes clear – his goal will be reached, and his suffering is over. Until then, he knows he must suffer because he does not yet see the One Who expended His blood to buy man's salvation and makes man holy through sprinkling with that blood.[9] The chief temptation of every Christian under trial is to imagine a heartless Father, a worthless Christ, and a weak Spirit, so Peter assures the

---

[6] The OT libation signifies the sanctification of God's people through the preaching of the Lamb's blood, Ap XXIV.36, per 1 Pet. 1.2.
[7] The commitment faith makes is difficult and indeed impossible for the godless, per 1.8, at Ap. XVIII.74.
[8] Faith is convinced that God is reconciled to us for Christ's sake, per 1.5, at Ap. III.265, and we remain in faith and boast in hope of glory because of faith alone per 1.5, 9 at FC SD IV.34.
[9] Life eternal pertains to faith as does justification according to 1.9 in Ap. III.233.

chosen saints of the Dispersion that the Father's heart is turned toward them. Christ's blood remains more precious than gold or silver, and the Spirit's power has revealed these truths and this power to them in these last days.[10]

This power is made known in the church through the Christians' love for one another. Under persecution, we are prone to be torn apart, biting, and devouring one another. Instead, Christians shall love one another since Christ has commanded it, and love will abide when everything else that is corruptible or temporary disappears. Though the apostles sometimes use different words and ways of presenting Christ's teachings, the essential unity of their teaching is due to its origin in Christ's own words: Who, when He was at the hour of trial and His death, commanded His disciples to love one another.

Chapter 2

Those things fitting for darkness must then be put aside. Christians lay aside whatever reeks of the night and its illusions: malice, deceit, slander, all those sins of tongue and heart that seem all right when no one is looking and will resound terribly when spoken from the housetops someday. In the light of Christ's resurrection, it is daytime now, and He works to build us into His new temple.[11] No temple is needed in Jerusalem now only because He builds His temple of His people wherever they are found and scattered. In that temple, all His people are priests; every priest is known through obedience to his Lord's Word.[12]

The priests of the Old Testament either taught the Law as God gave it or disobeyed Him through neglect of the Word – just so in the time of the New Testament in His blood. This priesthood is also a nation and a people – born not of blood as all the nations of the earth are but born from above water and the Spirit – and its constitution is His Word that the priesthood proclaims.[13] The word "proclaim" is the ground of the priesthood's activity – not the public ministry of the Word in the name of the church that Christ instituted through His apostles but the incessant use of God's Word in daily life with the family and with everyone we know. This priesthood is busy daily with the Word of God and those spiritual sacrifices of thanksgiving that now adorn this temple, which is His church.[14]

Such a priesthood is known through its obedience to Him, which is chiefly the rejection of one's passionate desires for what one does not have, those sins of the heart condemned from the First Commandment's denial of idolatry to the Tenth

---

10 The angels have their delight and joy (1·12) in looking into the personal union of Christ's two natures, this God-man Who shed His precious blood for us, FC SD VIII·30.
11 They who believe hearts may be cleansed without faith in Christ believe in a dream, 2·6, Ap. XII·65, and 2·6 agrees with Rom. 9·33 that on account of the merits of Christ are we accounted righteous when we believe in Him, Ap. XXI·31.
12 Peter urges us to come to Christ that we may be built upon Him, vv. 4-6, Ap. III·118.
13 NT sacrifices are eucharistic or sacrifices of praise according to 2·5, Ap XXIV·26, and our spiritual offerings are acceptable to God for Christ's sake, 2·5, FC SD VI·22.
14 2·9 attests that the church has been given the keys as it is a royal priesthood, Tr. 68.

Commandment's denial of covetousness.[15] The heart detached from one's passions is attached to God's Word. In a time of persecution, likely at the hands of some level of government, attachment to Christ will be known in subordination to the powers that be (Rom. 13:1) and recognition that those powers have their role of vengeance from God and their final accountability to God. Masters have the same, and if they are unjust, as powers often are, the Christian slaves under their command rejoice to suffer unjustly from the powers, as did the only true Master, the Lord Jesus. The Christians under government or earthly masters will be known through their conformity to the Lord's image of suffering under unjust powers.[16]

> The picture of God's people as a royal priesthood is a picture of activity, not passivity. The work of the priesthood is in active service as the priesthood of the Old Testament was busy with God's Word, with the worship of God, with the upkeep of the temple and its environs, and with ensuring that people knew the Word of God. Christians who are not ordained – sometimes called "the laity" or "parishioners" or "pew sitters" – cannot leave knowledge of Scripture or activity in God's kingdom to the "elders" or "teachers" or "bishops" – now most often called pastors. If pastors oversee kingdom work, all priests have a share in kingdom work now as much as they have an eternal share in God's kingdom.

Chapter 3

As in 1 Corinthians 7, wives whose husbands are not Christians are admonished to win their husbands through their conduct rather than their words. This situation can arise because the wife may be convicted through gospel preaching but cannot lead her husband to the same conviction through discussion or admonition. The New Testament does not discuss husbands similarly because it presumes the husband's Christianity is also his wife's since he is head of the household. Men's headship is not dealt with as the best option among other options but as a principle of how life works. Men and women relate to each other differently, and the husband is head of the household even when he is not a Christian. So, the wife's quiet and beautiful conduct affects her husband differently than the man's gentle and understanding way with his wife when she is overwhelmed (the most straightforward meaning of a "weaker vessel" that cannot hold all that another vessel might). The order of marriage – how it works and what its roles are – is ordered toward the leading of husband and wife both to Christ.[17]

Subordination to government and masters and grasping one's role in marriage are of a piece with all Christians' lives of blessing for blessing others with tenderheartedness and compassion rather than the evil and deceit that will not inherit the blessing laid up for the one who perseveres in the way of Jesus. Peter clearly asks why such suffering is good and answers just as clearly that when one suffers for having done evil, there is no blessing but only punishment. When one suffers for having followed Christ rather than men,

---

15 FC SD II-84 uses 2-11 to show that in the regenerate an obstinacy against the Word and will of God remains.

16 2-13ff in the Table of Duties shows what subjects owe to magistrates.

17 3-6 in the Table of Duties is addressed to wives, 3-7 to their husbands in the same document.

however, there is abundant blessing because then only do you suffer as a Christian – as a little Christ wronged but steadfast, receiving evil from men but through that suffering receiving goodness from God Himself.[18] As the men of old came into the ark to receive the Lord's salvation after the time of hardship had passed, we come into Baptism, a safe spot amid the deluge. Baptism provides a good conscience because it provides Christ, as our life in Him finds its goal in His inheritance. If we are with Him here and now through Baptism, we shall be with Him and see Him then and there in glory. Peter's call for subordination and love in all walks of life is a call back to the purity and clarity Baptism gives.

Chapter 4

The Christians are now God's Israel, so non-Christians are called here as elsewhere in the New Testament "Gentiles" (1 Cor. 5:1, 1 Thess. 4:5, 1 Pet. 2:12 and 4:3, 3 Jn. 7) but where Jews and Gentiles of old were identified through genealogy, true Israelites or true Jews and true Gentiles are distinguished through their ways of life. God's Israel lives in obedience to Him, not its own passions. The unbeliever lives in obedience to his own destructive passions, the works of darkness, and of the night that enslave him to Satan and to sin. Christ did not die so that we could be enslaved to sin. He died to free us from sin and its goal, death. He even descended to hell to announce His victory so that His triumph would be known to all flesh.[19]

That victory is the ground of the warning to be sober and watchful. Since Christ has conquered sin and death, He may return at any time. The church cannot live as if His coming is far off, as the Gentiles do, who claim that everything is going the way it always has, so there is no need for repentance or watchfulness. Our gifts used for His purposes and our sufferings in His image bear witness that we believe in His power and in His coming,[20] not in the foolish convictions of the flesh that will fade like the morning dew from the grass.[21] We live now as if Judgment Day is already here because at His resurrection it has indeed already begun, and the church's life under His Word confesses that one day all flesh will answer to Him. If life is hard for us for this short time, what will it be for the disobedient for all eternity?

Chapter 5

The shepherds or elders[22] of the church must live as Christ did in His ministry: for the benefit of the flock, not the benefit of self. They serve; they are not served. How often do the ministers of the church heed this teaching? If we do not desire to be paid in gold or silver, do we still not desire adulation and more attention? The shepherd is known

---

18 3·18 is an example of explaining the person of Christ according to what is ascribed to each nature, as here His suffering in the flesh, FC SD VIII·37.
19 4·1 is a similar speaking of the person according to the unique properties of one or the other nature, FC SD VIII·37.
20 The true meaning of 4·8 as love toward one's neighbor, not a propitiation for sin, explained in Ap. III·117.
21 The saints are also subject to death and all afflictions, 4·17, Ap. VI·54.
22 5·1 proves that bishops and elders are the same class of ministers, Tr. 62.

for his willingness, energy, and being an example to the flock. He is not recognized for the lazy accumulation of money, attention, or whatever else his passions may suggest to his unsteady mind.[23] The "younger people" are then not the young in age[24] but the "young" over against the church's elders or what we would call "the congregants" or "the parishioners" over against the pastor. Their humility and acceptance of the shepherd's guidance display the unique New Testament model of authority: the one in authority lives for the one under his authority, and the one under authority accepts that self-giving authority as good and very good. Authority is built into the relationship, and without authority, the relationship has no form or reality.

Satan would snatch away that authority to bless and to guide, as he would devour anything or anyone good or born of God and coming from God. Resistance to Satan is obedience to God.[25] God's work to sustain His saints through their trials – whether in Babylon, a codeword for Rome, or throughout the world, as all the brothers suffer for their faith – is the keynote of Peter's conviction: the One who will see you through the trial is the One who is mightier than the trial. The One who will sustain you to the end is the One with sole power over the end of all things.[26] Whether under trial and suffering or overwhelmed with blessing, the Christian stands through his Baptism in God's grace, safe and secure in the holy ark of the Christian Church, God's nation and people, His royal priesthood. No exile or affliction will take that away from His elect sprinkled with the precious blood of Christ.

The SECOND LETTER of PETER

AUTHOR

THOUGH sometimes disputed due to its resemblance to Jude's letter, this letter also clearly claims the apostle Peter as its author. We take the Holy Spirit at His Word and understand this to be Peter's second general letter to the church warning against dangers common to Christians.

---

23 5.3 forbids the bishops to be lords and to lord it over the churches, AC XXVIII·76-77.
24 The Small Catechism uses the verse differently. 5·5-6 are used in the Table to address young people in general concerning their duties.
25 5·2 demonstrates that the necessity of good works is a necessity of the ordinance of God's immutable will and of the creature's obedience to his Creator, FC SD IV·17.
26 God is so faithful that having begun a good work in us, He will see it to the end per 5·10, FC SD XI·32.

COMPOSITION AND PURPOSE

No specific occasion needs to be given for a letter admonishing Christians against unholiness and false teaching, the most frequent cancers that appear in the Body of Christ. This letter shares those two topics with all the general epistles, for what is generally threatening must be generally known and generally cut out from the Body before it threatens its soundness.

CONNECTIONS TO THE OLD AND NEW TESTAMENTS

Some of the same vocabulary and phrasing is found in this letter as in Jude's. This similarity may be traced back to the Lord's own descriptions of false teachers and their fruits and the vividness of speech He uses there. What is most dangerous must be seen so the language is strong and clear here as everywhere else, and Scripture warns about false teaching. The Old Testament is present as a source of images and examples rather than through extensive direct quotations.

OUTLINE

1:1-2	GREETINGS
1:3-21	TRUE TEACHING
2:1-22	FALSE TEACHING AND THE NATURE OF FALSE TEACHERS
3:1-18	CLEAR AND PRESENT DANGERS

CHAPTER 1

Like each of the general epistles, this second letter of Peter is addressed to all Christians in hard circumstances. The common concern of Peter, James, John, and Jude is that Christians should prove "barren or unfruitful" in difficult growing conditions – persecution, confusion, and the demands of the flesh that is bound for corruption. The specific problems of Paul's letters yield in the general letters to the common problem of the parable of the Sower: growth and flourishing are rare and remain God's gift from start to finish. Christians must always ask for much from the Good Giver because they are always in need.

Believers are alive in Christ and already "partakers of the divine nature" that do not die and are not subject to corruption and death.[27] They abide in that divine nature as they supplement what they have with Peter's growth pattern in 1:5-7. The connection between each quality is one step more between faith in Christ and love in Christ.[28] Based on faith, one moves from what one needs for himself – virtue and self-control, for example

---

27 If we ourselves are partakers of the divine nature according to 1-4, what kind of communion of the divine nature must there that God and man are one person? according to FC SD VIII-33-34.

28 1-10 teaches that good works preserve one's calling but do not merit remission of sins, Ap. XX-89-90; we should be very diligent to live according to God's will, FC Ep. XI-14. How to exhort to good works is well-modeled in 1-10, FC SD IV-33.

– to being needful to others – kind in a brotherly way and showing love. The link from faith to love is the beating heart of this letter as it is of all the general letters: the Christian and the church who have faith but have no love will not withstand the trials they undergo nor give any pleasing sound in their praises (cf. 1 Cor. 13).

That love has a goal whose nearness Peter senses in his own life. Soon, death will come, and at that moment, when love finds its Goal, an entrance is found for those who have persevered in Christ. Peter writes to ensure they endure all the dangers life presents to believers. As they walk, they must attend carefully to the Word of God because only it can guide them through the darkness. Life is dangerous and dark at the same time, so that one could kill you is also something you may never see in time. Since the path is narrow, steep, and slippery, the Christian must heed the Scriptures as the only light he has shining in this dark place until he enters the well-lit, spacious places of his eternal inheritance.[29]

Chapter 2

From that light, false teachers would drag you away. With them, you will find that eternal destruction that is their own goal and end, and through them, you become a partaker not of the divine nature's eternal life through Christ but of the divine nature's eternal wrath on sin apart from Christ.[30] In the days of Noah and each day since Genesis 3, there have been false teachers. They operate secretly because their foolishness and wickedness would be readily known if they were public. Like Satan, they must come in another guise than their true form. They are never what they seem at first. Like Satan, they are covetous, wanting what they do not have, never satisfied with what they do have. Lke Satan, their end is destruction.

They may be recognized through how they talk and through how they act. Their talk is like the bold blasphemies of the false teachers of the days of Noah and of Lot, not matched by the reticence of the holy angels who do not speak so boldly. What is the relationship to the angels? False teachers resemble the fallen angels, also called demons, in their presumption, willfulness, and fruitlessness. True teachers resemble holy angels in their humility, obedience to God, and fruitfulness in their service.

This is genuinely worse than if they had never known the gospel or been ordained to preach it because then they would have indulged their passions in their ignorance.[31] Greater blame is heaped on the teacher who leads not only himself through his passions of lust or greed into sin but also many others who had likewise escaped corruption, become partakers of the divine nature, but were turned through his lies back into slaves of unrighteousness.[32] For such a teacher, the verdicts of this chapter are too good, and

---

29 1·21 is proof that God wishes to deal with us through the external Word, SA III·IX, 10-13.
30 God and His election are not to blame for men's damnation. Only their own wickedness is the cause of their damnation, 2·1, FC Ep. XI·12, and Peter was right to state that there will be false teachers in the church, 2·1, Ap. XXIII·5.
31 With those who receive the Word and later reject it, their last state is worse than their first, 2·10, 20, FC SD XI·42, and Christ will punish those who willfully turn away from the holy commandment, 2·20, FC SD XI·83.
32 Peter predicted that there would be godless bishops, 2·13, Tr. 81.

the reality of his end in destruction will be far worse. It would have been better for him never to have been born.

Chapter 3

Scripture named in this chapter includes the Old Testament, the words that were already or would soon be written down in the gospels, and the letters of Paul. To all those, the believers must attend eagerly because there are many words abroad, rumors challenging the truth of God's promises and His justice, asserting that judgment will never come. Believers and unbelievers must recall that the world once formed from water was deluged by water, and this world now existing will be consumed by fire day.[33] Believers do not look for this world to endure forever as do unbelievers, but for new heavens and new earth without Adam's stain upon it all, without death, incorruptible like their resurrection bodies.

The believer's goal will arrive on that day of incorruptibility and eternal life. For it, he looks, and onward to it, he presses. Some twist even the apostle Paul's words to deceive the believer, but he will not be dissuaded from the prize of God's day of righteousness and life. Rather than being turned to wickedness by falsehood, he will grow in the grace and knowledge of Christ, the gift and the wisdom going together in the believer's life as faith and love go and grow together. One day, faith will find its fulfillment in sight, such as the preview of Christ's resurrection that Peter, James, and John had on the holy mountain. Until that day, the Word that endures is the Word that guides and preserves through every trial. On that day, love that never passes away will find its completion in the One Who makes all things new.

The FIRST LETTER *of* JOHN

AUTHOR

The writer of this letter, and the two after it, is the same author of the Fourth Gospel and the Revelation of the Lord Jesus Christ. Protests to the contrary make little sense of the overlap of word choice, imagery, and tone between the gospel, the letters, and the apocalypse. This beloved disciple is writing with customary intimacy of the things he had seen, felt, heard, and touched concerning the Lord in Whose bosom he reclined at the Last Supper.

---

33 On 3·9, there is much· true judgment concerning predestination must be learned solely from the holy Gospel concerning Christ, FC Ep. XI·10; the promise of the gospel is universal, FC SD XI·28; God's faithfulness will see to its end the work He has begun in us, FC SD XI·32; all preparation for condemnation is by the devil and man, through sin, and in no respect to God, FC SD XI·81; God will punish those who turn away from His holy commandment, FC SD XI·83.

COMPOSITION AND PURPOSE

Like the other general epistles, John's three letters are intended for immediate and wide circulation. The dangers discussed and the remedies provided are all very general, especially concerning the coherence of the congregation and the lovelessness and attachment to one's passions that could threaten any local church. The apostle desires Christians to stick together despite the allurements of a world that persecutes the church and entices Christians to give up the fire of their "first love" (Rev. 2:4).

CONNECTIONS TO THE OLD AND NEW TESTAMENTS

John does not quote the Old Testament directly or frequently in his letters. Like his gospel, his letters use the words of the Old Testament, particularly concerning sacrifice and the words of the Lord Jesus. Those words form a clear pattern of words about sin, love, sacrifice, God's Lamb, commandment, and many others. As John always does, those words are immediately recognizable when placed next to each other. So, the connection to the rest of the New Testament is very directly to the other writings of John and only indirectly to the other gospels or letters, as John has kept his own stream of tradition that provides us with the fullest possible picture of Jesus and His teachings. Important among that tradition for this letter is Jesus' admonition to love one another in connection with foot washing, humility, and His betrayal and death. To that commandment of love always old and always new, the apostle returns time and again.

OUTLINE

1:1-4	THE APOSTOLIC WITNESSES
1:5-2:2	PURIFICATION FOR COMMUNION
2:3-17	THE LIFE OF COMMUNION
2:18-29	DANGERS TO COMMUNION WITH CHRIST
3:1-24	WHO GOD'S CHILDREN ARE
4:1-6	THE SPIRIT AND HIS TRUTH
4:7-21	THE NATURE AND POWER OF LOVE
5:1-5	FAITH OVERCOMING
5:6-20	GOD'S WITNESS AND OUR CONFIDENCE IN HIM

CHAPTER 1

All Christian life flows from Christ's life. If He were not alive, if the apostles had not heard and seen and touched that Life as Thomas put his finger in the Lord's side and all of them breakfasted on the shore, then sin and fellowship and the other things that will arise in John's letters would matter little. The fact that the living Jesus was manifested to the apostles means that the practice of sin has no place in the Christian's life, as darkness, lying, and self-deception have no place. Instead, the reality of Christ's life means that light, truth, and confession of sin take the place of all those things. We walk in His light along the path He has marked for us. We know Him, Who is the Truth, and speak the truth ourselves. We confess our sins rather than allow them to become a habit because the blood of the living Christ cleanses us.[34]

There are several possibilities in anyone's life any day of his life. John spells them out so we understand their foolishness, e.g., claiming fellowship with Christ while going about our lives ("walking") without Him and His Word. He also spells out what life is if we are honest and speak the truth about God and ourselves, e.g., if we confess our sins, God will forgive our sins and cleanse us again.[35] These possibilities of life – life in the light or in the darkness, a life of truth or lies, of cleansing or filth – John will explore and explain throughout the letter.

> *This first chapter of John's first letter reminds us of the ground of the whole New Testament: living men saw and were commissioned to preach the living Christ risen from the dead. Without that witness, there would be no New Testament, as there would be no Old Testament without the witness of the prophets. Christianity is not a religion of blind faith in something we hope proves true. Ours is a religion founded on eyewitnesses to that Man Whom they knew had died and been buried and yet Whom they saw alive after three days.*

CHAPTER 2

Christ is not a Savior only in theory. If anyone does sin – a term John uses for the ongoing practicing and cherishing of one's sins rather than for all infractions against God's Law – Christ is not a theoretical Mediator. His blood is the grounds of God's propitiation – His being pleased and satisfied with us – and the means of our reconciliation to the Father. Once one realizes that the reality of Christ's body being killed in our place and rising from the dead for our life drives John's thinking, you can see why the apostle is so practical. If Christ's work were shuffling some papers or numbers around, our lives would be just as untouched by God's Word as we sometimes think.[36] Since His blood was really shed to cleanse us, everything about our lives is changed.[37]

John's concerns are always practical.[38] In his letter, you find the unity between faith and love, between confessing the truth and living in truth, evident in the Lord's practical words to His disciples, "If you love Me, keep My commandments." (John 14:15) You can

---

34   1·7 is key to the articles of sin, of righteousness, and of election· sin cannot be the same thing as man because God cleanses us from sin, FC SD I·45; our righteousness defined as the person of Christ with His work on our behalf as described in 1·7, FC SD III·57; communication of attributes predicated also of the human nature that has divine power, FC SD VIII·59; preaching of the gospel is universal, FC SD XI·28.

35   1·8 means no person can bear God's judgment, Ap. III·39; no glory of righteousness for any if God does not forgive, Ap. III·208; if sin has its way then the Holy Ghost and faith are not present, SA III·IV, 44.

36   The promise of the remission of sins requires faith, 2·12, Ap. III·152.

37   True judgment concerning predestination must be learned alone from the gospel of Christ, 2·2, FC SD XI·10; gospel preaching is universal, FC SD XI·28.

38   2·1 means that in all afflictions we should call on God and no other, AC XXI.

hear the slogans of people who can explain to themselves and others why they persist in their sin but say, "I know Him." There is no space for theoretically knowing God and practically denying His commandment to love one another. By such practice, a person denies the One Who walked in love. We walk as He walked, lest we deny that He walked in love for us.

The church is pictured in all of John's letters as a family: the brother is loved, and the members are little children or young men or fathers, each with blessings specific to his position in the body. To the apostle, the whole church comprises "little children" whom he loves and admonishes to walk in Christ's truth. This warmth and closeness are the Lord's warmth and closeness with the Twelve and with John, especially, who was nearest Jesus among those Twelve. In that family, the possibility that you would hate your brother is impossible because of the facts of what Christ had done. Look at the past tense verbs of vv. 12-14. We have been forgiven, have known God, have overcome the wicked one, and have known the Father. Those realities in Christ drive the admonition on either side of those verses to love the brother and not to be deceived by the world's allurements. We live in this way because it is the Way Christ shows us, the only Way where we have forgiveness, knowledge of God, victory over Satan, and knowledge that God is truly our Father for Christ's sake.

The world – all that is opposed to God – is in the process of extinction, but its deceptive allurements still call to us. If we follow that call, we will be bitterly disappointed in time, even when that call resounds in the church. "Antichrist" is used in John's letters for anyone in the church opposed to the teaching of Christ, in this case, and in his other letters, particularly people who deny that Jesus Christ came in the flesh, that is, who deny the Lord's incarnation. Such denial, of course, lets one off the hook in loving the brother because if Christ did not come in the flesh to love us, we need not love anyone in the flesh. Such denials of Christ were and are abroad in the church and outside the church, claiming you can be a Christian without believing that Christ is the only Son of the Father.

These antichrists departed from John's fellowship, a salutary church split. Their departure followed from their false doctrine, and John was ready to have them gone since they denied the fundamentals of the faith. The Christians need not be deceived: their infilling with the Holy Spirit, their "anointing," has given them the ability to understand these things, not to be shaken by the departures, to know what God's commandment of love is, and to practice it. John's letter is for recalling that anointing and strengthening his "little children" in the walk Christ has given them.

Chapter 3

As in the Lord's last teaching to His disciples on the night He was betrayed, love is this chapter's sum and capstone. In it, we see the goal of His wisdom given to us and the measure of our life in Him with our brothers. If we lack it, it proves a lack of much else,[39] and when we have it, we need nothing more. In this way, love is evergreen, an old commandment we heard at the beginning of our life in Christ and a new commandment fresh every morning with its joys.

We know what love is because He is Who He is and does what He does. We cannot define love outside of the love the Father bestowed on us, like a man giving gifts to his children. And with Him, giving gifts is always more than we can ask or imagine because there is always more to be given. For now, we have the knowledge of God in Christ Jesus, the reality that He has come to destroy the works of Satan, including the deception of Adam that led us into sin through false teaching,[40] and that He has given His Spirit to abide with us.[41] John's words here recall and repeat Jesus' words in the Last Supper teaching over and again, down to their pattern of coming back to the same idea again from a slightly different angle each time.

This present knowledge purifies us for a day when our knowledge will be perfect, not partial. Right now, the world does not recognize the love we know or our love because it does not know or have Christ. We are like Him in this obscurity and will be like Him when we see Him. Since that Day of seeing is coming, we are diligent now to follow His way: to love the brothers, confess our sins, and give up ourselves for the brothers as Christ did for His friends. No recognition from the world follows from our love, and all love is made of actions rather than feelings. Love is not a feeling. Love is the work Christ has given us to do, and it goes with and comes from faith. These two things go together in God's teaching: belief in Christ Jesus and love of the brothers.[42]

Chapter 4

If the world does not know or heed Christ and His Christians, it does know and heed false teachers. False teaching can be recognized through its content – in this case, denying that Christ came in the flesh – and through its effect – the praise it receives from the world. The content and the effect go together; by them, we can recognize the "antichrist," the one putting himself in the place of and opposite Christ, and the "spirit of error." We know the Spirit of truth, the Holy Spirit, through how God's truth is frequently repeated and creates faith and love through His teaching.[43]

Why is the love of the brothers so often stressed? Because the brother is everyone, we are most prone to neglect. The one close to home is the easiest to hate because we know him so well, and the easiest to neglect because he is always there. We always see him, while God is harder to hate and easier to love since we do not see Him. It seems the brother makes all the demands on our time, and God, Who is now invisible, demands little to nothing.

The apostle makes clear that God desires love not for Himself alone but for

---

39 Per 3·9, if sin has its way then the Holy Ghost and faith are not present, SA III·IV, 44.
40 By Satan's instigation of one man, sin entered the world, 3·7, FC SD I·7.
41 By divine aid we might overcome through faith in Christ, 3·8, Ap. III·18.
42 One who does not love surely is not justified but is still in death, 3·14, FC SD III·27.
43 Faith precedes and love follows per 4·19, Ap. III·20.

Himself through the brother. He commands us to love the brother because He knows our proneness to convenient forgetting. We easily need to remember what is hardest and move on to what we imagine are better things. Instead, He would have our love focused on the one nearest and often hardest to love and would keep it there.[44] Through such love we abide with Him as He abides with us through the Holy Spirit Whom He has given to us: this abiding and this love on either side not at all the easiest thing in the world but a difficult making of our homes with each other that will be worth it in the End.

Chapter 5

Prayer and confidence are choked out through sin. The sin of hating the brother keeps us apart from him and through separation from him apart, too, from God. The assurance that we know God and that His commandments are not burdensome is an invitation to draw near to the brother and with the brother near to God. The doubtful portion of v. 7 concerning the three persons of the Trinity is not almost any Greek manuscript of the New Testament [footnote here] is not needful to the apostle's point. The point of God's closeness and how we know Him to be close through the Spirit Who abides with us, the water of rebirth in Baptism, and the blood of Christ shed on the cross and given in the Supper is abundantly clear. We know Him to be near through faith in His Word, and we love those who are near according to His Word.

The certainty of His witness – His utter truthfulness and the confirmations of His testimony without number – drives our confidence in prayer and the throwing down of idols. We can know Him to be listening and to be ready to answer our prayer because we know Who He is. Even the most grievous sins of the brother can be turned to prayers for the brother's repentance. Not all sin heads in the same direction. The sin against the Holy Spirit, what John calls "sin leading to death," rejects the source of forgiveness and grace in the Spirit's giving of Christ and has no remedy. If a brother commits that sin, our prayer avails nothing, and the brother will be lost, whatever we think or say. That is not in our hands. We cannot know that the brother will finally be lost, so our prayer is always that he may be saved and his sins covered and cleansed through Christ's blood. For the brother, we pray because we always hope in Christ.[45]

Idols are the creation of men's hands, but before that, they are the works of men's

> The worship of false gods happens uncommonly in the form of images and statues. Some cultures make those images, statues, and other depictions of their gods. Some do not, as the traditional religion of Japan, Shinto, does not. All cultures – including ones outwardly Christian – make idols commonly in the human heart. Avoidance of idolatry means cleansing the heart and its continual renewal through the Word of God. We study God's Word and have our hearts refreshed because idolatry is always ready to defile our hearts with its filth. Keeping ourselves from idolatry is keeping ourselves in the Word of God.

---

44 The Scriptures say in many places as also in 4·21 that works are necessary and that we must and ought to do them because of "God's ordinance, command, and will," FC SD IV·14.
45 God gives us eternal life for a certainty only for Christ's sake, 5·12, Ap. III·212.

hearts. The heart leads the hand to do what it does and the tongue to say what it says. There will be no idolatry if the heart is cleansed through faith in Christ. If the heart is wrapped up in and enticed by other gods and the world's allurements, then idols will multiply beyond counting.[46] John's final admonition to keep ourselves from idols is like all his teachings to faith in Christ, Whose day is coming quickly, and to love for the brothers who will meet that day with us. By idolatry, the heart is trapped to hate the brother and to deny the Christ. By true teaching and the Spirit of Truth, the heart is enraptured to love the brother and believe in the Christ Whom God has sent for our salvation, not ours only, but the salvation of the whole world.

The SECOND LETTER *of* JOHN

AUTHOR

THE writer of this letter, and the two after it, is the same author of the Fourth Gospel and the Revelation of the Lord Jesus Christ. Protests to the contrary make little sense of the overlap of word choice, imagery, and tone between the gospel, the letters, and the apocalypse. This beloved disciple is writing with customary intimacy of the things he had seen, felt, heard, and touched concerning the Lord in Whose bosom he reclined at the Last Supper.

COMPOSITION AND PURPOSE

This second letter is directed to an unnamed Christian church and her members, pictured as "the elect lady and her children," concerning a general problem for all Christian churches: false teaching and false teachers. Its origin is, therefore, obscure because it could have been written at any point in the apostle's ministry. By tradition, he is believed to have lived into old age and did not die in martyrdom. It might have been written between the 40s and the 90s of the first century AD. Its general applicability to all Christian churches of all times and places exhibits the stress that God places on the purity of Christian teaching and its deep connection to love for a pure faith founded on pure doctrine begets pure love.

---

46 On 5·10, the promise of God should and only can be received by faith, Ap. III·176; if the heart doubts, it denies the truth of God's promise of forgiveness, Ap. XII·62; if anyone doubts, he charges the divine promise with falsehood, Ap. XII·88.

CONNECTIONS TO THE OLD AND NEW TESTAMENTS

The false teachers who are itinerant as were the Old Testament prophets and New Testament apostles show a continuity between the testaments in the life of God's people. Some men bring true teaching, some bring false, and the congregation of the believers must always discern the true from the false, the Spirit of God from the antichrist.

OUTLINE

1-3	GREETING
4-6	WALKING IN TRUTH
7-11	FALSE TEACHERS
12-13	CONCLUSION

Though John wrote in his first letter to the entire church of Christ, he writes in this letter to an anonymous church addressed symbolically as "the elect lady and her children." This could be a household, but it is strange that he should call one Christian woman "elect" and not her children as well as her fellow congregants. Like the letters in John's Revelation, this letter uses picture language to show the church as a woman with a house full of children like the mother church of Galatians 4:26. The church from which the apostle writes is "your elect sister with her children," all churches pictured here as fruitful mothers upon whom God's blessing rests. The plural of v. 8 reveals many addressed in addressing "the lady," so the admonitions of this letter and its reminders are for the whole church, not a particular woman. An elder in Christ[47] – what we now call a pastor – writes to a church about the dangers to the family of God.

Those admonitions are not new: watch for deceivers and love the children of God. Why, then, this letter in addition to the first one of John? Deceivers work against the individual Christian's soul and the church at large, asking to be received into the church's care and attention when they should not be. The believers in this church should watch for one who comes without bringing the teaching of Who Jesus is. He pretends to teach of the Father without teaching of the Son. Such a one should not be welcomed. There are limits to Christian kindness. Kindness is good with truth, but without truth, kindness would let Satan himself preach in the church. Not to allow a deceiver into the church and not even to greet such a deceiver is to love God and His teaching and His Christ more than you love your sense of being nice or kind. It is imperative for Christians to love God above all things.

To love God is also to love each other in the church. Walking in this commandment will prove a bulwark against the world's deceptions since a body united in the truth cannot so easily be deceived as a body divided up already for a wolf to pick off one by one. John's preference for speaking face-to-face in this letter of very average length for an ancient

---

47 John calls himself an elder at 2 Jn 1, Treatise 62, proving that elders are the ministers of the church, and the apostles such as John were among the number of the ministers of the divine Word.

letter is a preference for those face-to-face relationships no writing can replace and where deception finds no room. He would speak with the Christians how they shall one day see their Master: not distant, not hard to scope out, but right there, plain as day, right in front of your face. If His teachings and the actions we should take because of them are somewhat hard to understand at times and there is much deception in the world, that day will reveal everything with clarity and plainness. Deception and deceivers in the church will then be shown openly to be what even now we sense they are: antichrists. The truth will then be proven altogether true, as we know it to be by faith.

The THIRD LETTER of JOHN

AUTHOR

The writer of this letter, and the two after it, is the same author of the Fourth Gospel and the Revelation of the Lord Jesus Christ. Protests to the contrary make little sense of the overlap of word choice, imagery, and tone between the gospel, the letters, and the apocalypse. This beloved disciple is writing with customary intimacy of the things he had seen, felt, heard, and touched concerning the Lord in Whose bosom he reclined at the Last Supper.

COMPOSITION AND PURPOSE

This pastoral letter addresses a man named Gaius, a common Roman name, who must understand the errors of a minister named Diotrephes and the goodness of an otherwise rejected minister named Demetrius. Rejection of a teacher and the refusal to help him along in his ministry is a rejection of his teaching, whether that teaching is true or false. If the teaching is true, rejection of the teacher is a rejection of the divine teaching he brings. Christians such as Gaius must learn to discern truth from falsehood, from the words of the truth spoken even by humble Demetrius, and from the evil actions of haughty Diotrephes.

CONNECTIONS TO THE OLD AND NEW TESTAMENTS

There is a deep connection to the reception of prophets into the homes of some and the protection of prophets in times of persecution with the "man of peace" Jesus predicted His disciples would find as they went into the villages and towns of Galilee, Judea, and Samaria. Reception of the man is a reception of his teaching, and if the teaching he brings is the teaching of Jesus, then he who accepts that man accepts Jesus, too. The connections to other portions of Scripture in 3 John are then connections of action per the focus on deeds and behavior John has.

OUTLINE

1	Greeting
2-8	Commendation and instructions concerning hospitality
9-10	The evils of Diotrephes' conduct
11-12	Commendation of Demetrius

This letter to a fellow Christian concerns the workings of the ministry in the earliest church. As in his second letter, the apostle calls himself an "elder," a term equivalent to the term "bishop" in Paul's pastoral letters, and the doings of pastors and how the church can foster the gospel are the central themes of this brief letter. The joy John has in hearing of his "children" walking in the truth is the joy of hearing that they receive ministers of Christ traveling among the churches and will reject deceivers who are known for their love of "preeminence."

What do these things have to do with the more prominent teachings of the gospels and John's other letters? Deception, a constant theme in all of John's writing, is known here through Diotrephes' love of being first in everything, contrary to the way of Christ, Who thought He was first put Himself last for our sakes. To live in the love of preeminence is to imitate evil, not good. The church imitates good when it imitates God in Christ, receiving the truth and the proclaimers of the truth. How the church treats the ministers – receiving some who proclaim truth and rejecting others who do not – demonstrates how it does or does not understand God's teaching. Behavior is a matter of the confession of truth.

Demetrius' good testimony comes from the rest of the church, not from himself or John alone. The practice of fellowship among the churches is the practice of a unified voice concerning God's truth and the truthfulness of His ministers. Through receiving, we are united with each other. Through rejecting, we make clear who is not united with us. No Christian can live apart from other Christians, and Gaius' Christianity is known through how he receives the brothers who come in Christ's name, just as Jesus predicted of His sheep. No church can truly be "nondenominational" or "independent" because it cannot avoid receiving proclaimers or rejecting others, and its behavior, like the arrogance of Diotrephes, will display its grasp of Christ's truth.

The LETTER of JUDE

AUTHOR

This second brother of our Lord (Matt. 13:55, Mk. 6:3) to author a New Testament epistle speaks briefly and concisely, as do his brother Jesus and his brother James. A familial characteristic of laconic speech and even of silence when possible (cf. Matt. 2, where Joseph does not speak at all) is likely the cause of the brevity of this pointed letter.

COMPOSITION AND PURPOSE

A general epistle is generally meant and generally sent. This letter has no specific occasion apart from the widespread problem of false teaching coming into the church through the preaching office. Ministers are most often the cause of deception in the church since their voices resound the most. The Lord's brother warns that such deception is easily spotted in the behavior of the false teachers, beyond which the believers need look no further.

CONNECTIONS TO THE OLD AND NEW TESTAMENTS

Quotations of the Old Testament and from the apocryphal book of 1 Enoch are both quotations from ancient sources, and here, the apocryphal book is recognized as true as far as it goes in describing the humility of the angels. The allusions to Old Testament stories assume the readers' or hearers' familiarity with those stories as infamous examples of the wickedness of men who have abandoned the faith once delivered to the saints in exchange for their passions. More obvious are the connections to the letter of James and the teaching of Jesus, especially in the Sermon on the Mount, which piles up very lively images of how false teachers behave and what their rewards shall be for their manifold wickedness. This letter is drawn directly from the same source as the gospels: the words of the Lord Jesus Himself.

OUTLINE

1-2	Greeting
3-4	Why the letter has been written
5-7	Admonitions from the past
8-19	The reality and nature of ungodly teachers
20-23	The duties and delights of the believers
24-25	Praise of God

"Our common salvation" and the dangers false teachers present to it is so great and so frequent a theme among the general letters that some have assumed this letter of Jude to be somewhat a facsimile of the second letter of Peter. Far from it: common themes, common words, and common warnings are evidence of common problems. Believers in churches throughout the world face a common Enemy who has a limited set of tactics that always involve deception and lies. They should then be unsurprised when two apostles of the same Lord speak similarly since no trial has overtaken any believer or church that is not common to man. The men who creep in unnoticed in Jude creep in secretly in 2 Peter. Nothing changes about lying and evil, so the message of goodness and the Truth Himself does not change.

The Old Testament is the constant pattern for understanding truth and falsehood for the New Testament church. In the Old Testament, the wicked always seek a domain or order that is not their own, grasping something that does not belong to them or that is not theirs to do. The unbelieving Israelites who fell in the wilderness, the fallen angels, and the men of Sodom and Gomorrah are alike in their indulgence of the flesh and their end in destruction. These examples all show the way not to go; however, fervently wicked men admonish you to walk that way.

Likewise, false teachers today always resemble Cain, Balaam, and Korah, all false prophets in their boldness to defy godly authority and their freedom to speak of things they do not know. The holy angels are not so: Michael did not himself rebuke the wicked angels who sought Moses' body but called the Lord to punish wickedness rather than seek vengeance for himself. That scene of Michael is taken from the apocryphal book of 1 Enoch, like vv. 14-15 shows that the Holy Spirit uses information from many sources in the Scriptures, but unlike 1 Enoch, the letter of Jude is utterly reliable in all it says because the Spirit is its Author, whereas 1 Enoch may or may not be true since it has only a human being for its author. The difference between Scripture and everything else, even books that purport to be scriptural, is between the whole truth and something partly true. Hold to what is wholly true, and you won't go wrong.

Each description of false teachers layers detail upon detail so that the church can recognize more easily who is false in their midst: they come to the Communion table without fear and serve only themselves there; all their works like clouds on a dry day, fruitless trees, and seafoam result in nothing; they at once grumble incessantly and flatter incessantly, perhaps complaining secretly about the same people they praise openly; they mock and cause division and do not have God's Spirit. Knowing their words and their ways and comparing those to the Word of God are what the believers must do to avoid "those who cause divisions" (Rom. 16:17) whose ways are more fully explained here.

There can be no "heresy hunting" here because the false teacher is not like a prey animal - readily known and easily pursued. He pretends to be what he is not, as does a wolf in sheep's clothing. His disguise or mask must be pulled off if he is to be truly revealed. The apostles' words here, understood already as Holy Scripture, guide the believer in seeing who is false and practicing what is true, especially that love is the end and goal of the Christian's life. The plucking of the tempted and dying from the fires of destruction is love because it steers life toward Christ's mercy instead of the eternal fires prepared for the devil, his angels, and all who love their ways. On that day of judgment, the believer finds mercy because mercy triumphs over judgment for those whose lives are measured by love, not by the self-seeking of the false and the wicked.

The Revelation of St. John the Divine

The REVELATION *of* St. JOHN *the* DIVINE

AUTHOR

THE author is the evangelist and elder of the churches, James's brother, and Jesus's friend. Efforts to distance the author of the Apocalypse from the Evangelist and the Letter-writer of the rest of the New Testament contradict the coherence of the books' vocabularies and phrasing, the testimony of the ancient church, and the simple reality that a book would not obtain wide circulation without apostolic origin. John the Apostle is the authorizing figure of the book, and the vision of Christ's ultimate victory over evil is his eternal theme.

COMPOSITION AND PURPOSE

The setting of John's apocalypse is heavily debated and depends on whether one believes he is speaking in code about the Roman emperor Nero. Since that code depends on reckoning in Aramaic rather than the Greek in which he wrote, it is unlikely that it describes that emperor's reign or possible future resurrection as some pagans believed. The other popular option for the Apocalypse's date is the later reign of the emperor Domitian. Since we understand the book to symbolize the church's life now and its destiny in everlasting life, we need to attach no particular significance to any emperor's reign relative to the book. The churches of Asia Minor had already been founded, so Paul's ministry of the 40s and 50s into the early 60s was already past. The decline that had been so steep in the life of the Ephesians, whom Paul also addressed, must permit some time to pass between the apostle's ministry and the Apocalypse's letter to the same church. It may have been written as early as the mid-60s, and it does not mention the fall of the Jerusalem temple, so it likely predates that event in 70.

The purpose of the entire Apocalypse aligns its visions of destruction and renewal with its very practical letters: to strengthen the saints and to confirm them in the testimony of Christ Jesus, the King of Kings. It serves the same purpose for the church today. It is not material for wild speculation but sober, strong teaching building up God's church in her first Love.

CONNECTIONS TO THE OLD AND NEW TESTAMENTS

Revelation cites the Old Testament constantly and patterns John's vision on the visions of the prophets such as Ezekiel and Zechariah. The animals and creatures-stranger-than-animals one sees in this Apocalypse have their precursors in Daniel and Ezekiel. Revelation is incomprehensible without knowledge of the Old Testament, so the end of the book leads us back to and through its own beginning. The New Testament is most clearly linked to the Apocalypse through John's gospel and his other letters, where images such as the Lamb of God and of purification multiply until they are also found in Revelation.

OUTLINE

1:1-20	BLESSINGS AND WARNINGS
2:1-3:22	SEVEN LETTERS TO THE SEVEN CHURCHES
4:1-11	THE VISION OF GOD
5:1-14	THE VISION OF CHRIST
6:1-8:1	THE SEVEN SEALS
8:2-13:18	THE SEVEN TRUMPETS
14:1-20	WORSHIP AND JUDGMENT I
15:1-18:24	THE SEVEN BOWLS
19:1-20:15	WORSHIP AND JUDGMENT II
21:1-22:21	NEW CREATION, NEW JERUSALEM, AND ADMONITIONS

CHAPTER 1

The book was given to John as a revelation, an unveiling, not a veiling. Many see this book as dark and strange – it was written to be the very opposite. It brings light to a church afflicted for the sake of Christ so that they will know what "must soon take place" (1:1), the things Jesus is doing and shall do to bring righteousness to a world full of unrighteousness. The blessing of 1:5 mirrors the promise of 22:17 that the one who listens to this revelation of the Lord will find strength and comfort in times of need and at the end of time.

Though profitable for the whole church for all of time, the book is sent initially to seven churches in what is now Turkey, seven letters comprising a match to the seven letters of the General Epistles, fourteen in all to mirror Paul's fourteen (counting Hebrews as Paul's). Those seven letters come from the Son of Man, Whom John sees in His risen, reigning glory as One standing with His people amid the fire like the Son of God with the three young men in Daniel 3:25. The King of the world of Daniel 7:9-10, 13-14 is the same Son of God Who saw the young men through persecution. He will see His church now through its tribulation. Already in this chapter, we see the depth and beauty of Revelation's use of the Old Testament, all of it pointing to Christ and in Christ to a glorious future for His body, the Church.

This chapter finally establishes that the visions John is shown will be symbolic so that one thing stands for another: the stars are the church's angels or messengers (the same word in Greek), and the lampstands are the churches themselves. Most misunderstand this Apocalypse because they will not let it say what it wants to say in the way it wants to speak. One thing stands for another. No symbol is attached when something is plain, such as the vision of the Son of Man in this chapter. When something is figurative or symbolic, as the numbers and signs will be, the symbol is given and elsewhere taken up as we will see throughout the book.

Chapter 2

Each of the four churches in this chapter has problems that the Lord addresses through John, but no church has a problem unknown to anyone else. No congregation is unique in the threats to its faithfulness and its existence. Thus, every letter starts with Christ's assurance that He has the power to

> *The Apocalypse uses symbols, as do many places in the Holy Scriptures, to portray what is otherwise unknowable or invisible to mankind: the war of heaven upon Satan and his minions. This is why symbols come into use in places such as Ezekiel or Daniel, where that war is especially frequently portrayed, and why there are few to no symbols in straightforward histories such as the books of Samuel or the gospels. Where invisible things are in hand, symbols show our weak spiritual sight of the truths of God and His warfare for our sake. This is true for present conflicts, such as the struggles in Revelation 12, and future glories, such as the New Jerusalem in Revelation 21. The symbols are for our comfort, not our confusion.*

help and to punish, to know the church's woes and its joys because His work and ways are all-important for any congregation, and He is ruling over His church with the same direct knowledge and involvement we imagine any church official might. But rather than discussing church officials, structures, or politics, He directly discusses His ways and commandments with His people, for He rules His people directly through His Word.

The Ephesians have endured many things but departed from the love for Christ that they had at first. If they do not change their tune and come back to that love, their church will close since the removal of their lampstand (2:5) is the closure of a church, which is a lampstand (1:20). Church closure comes from the failure to repent, to change, and to turn back to Christ Who offers food from the tree of life to a repentant congregation (2:7).

The Smyrnaeans have faced persecution from the Jews, as did many early Christians, and have still more suffering at hand in imminent imprisonment (2:10). Tribulation is not a far-off possibility for them. It is a present and future reality (2:10). The crown laid up for them if they endure these things is the crown of athletic victory for which Paul also strove. The Christians who endure persecution and affliction now will one day thus be victors or conquerors (2:7, 10, 17, 26, 3:5, 12, 21), just as Paul predicted. The Christian life is an Olympic struggle, and the one who survives is an Olympic victor, worthy of the highest prize.

The Pergamonians lived in a city with a large temple of Zeus, likely the "throne of Satan" mentioned in 2:13. Despite the popularity of paganism, they do not deny Christ but do tolerate false prophecy like Balaam's, and false prophecy is recognized through their fellowship in the table of demons and their sexual immorality. The confluence of fellowship with demons and sexual immorality is visible throughout Scripture in both Christian and pagan environments. Eating what has been devoted to demons results in a life without self-control. Still, if one forsakes the demons' table, God will feed him with "hidden manna" (1:17) in this wilderness and destroy all false prophecies, even the sort tolerated in the church (2:15).

The Thyatirids have a very similar problem to the church in Pergamum. They tolerate a woman figuratively named "Jezebel" like the pagan wife of King Ahab because her immorality and unrepentant heart are leading the entire church astray as Jezebel in the Old Testament led the northern kingdom into further idolatry and unrighteousness. Christ promises that He will punish her and her disciples (her "children" in 2:23) with sickness and death if they do not repent. Not all in Thyatira have shared her teachings, and they must hold to what He taught them. Christians who conquer through Christ will reign with Him, ruling with a rod of iron over the nations (compare 2:27 to Ps. 2:8).

CHAPTER 3

The Sardians have a good reputation among the churches but little else. Christ knows much more about them than the judgments of other men could ever know. Therefore, He commands them to hold fast to what they have already heard. Christianity is a religion of the source. We always return to the pure, clear fountain of Israel – the Holy Scriptures – never waiting for some unknown future in which God will tell or show us something completely new. If someone refuses to return to the source of life, his name will be blotted out of Christ's book of life (3:5), as men who disgraced their cities in the ancient world had their names and images destroyed, never to be remembered anymore.

The Philadelphians are weak but faithful and suffer from persecution at the hands of the Jews, as do the Smyrnaeans. One day, all will acknowledge that the true Messiah of Israel loves believers, not only people who are ethnically Jewish, as many Jews then and now imagine. The interplay of holding fast to Christ and Christ holding fast to us is clearest for this church because Christ promises that He will stand with them as they have stood with Him. Loyalty is the hallmark of Christianity under fire. The one loyal to Christ will find Him utterly loyal through all things and at the last. He never abandons His friends.

Like the Ephesians, the Laodiceans had received a letter from the apostle Paul and another letter of Christ through the apostle John. The Laodiceans, like the Ephesians, have grown cold, but in their case, not cold enough because their temperature is lukewarm, such as room-temperature stuff that disgusts – ice cream that's too hot and a steak that's too cold. They imagine that they are doing well, but Christ shows the well-clothed to be naked and the rich to be very poor. They are commanded to purchase what they need from Him: gold that can withstand fire and garments to cover their shame. This will all come as news to them. Unlike some of the other letters among the seven, this one informs people who imagine themselves doing all right that they are unready for what stands before them. To each congregation, the Lord gives what it needs: a true Shepherd of His people, Israel, just as He has promised to be.

Chapter 4

Christ reigns amid tribulation. Before the destiny of nations and the church unfolds in his eyes, John is given a vision of Christ being enthroned, ruling in calm over a world in constant turmoil. Whatever is shaken or roiling, Christ is seated and ruling for the good of His body, the church. "What must take place" (4:1) is premised on the enthroned King. He is surrounded by precious jewels, as was paradise in the beginning and as the New Jerusalem will be in the end. Twenty-four elders also surround him, the leaders of Israel, old and new, patriarchs and apostles, and around Him is the perfection of God's sevenfold Spirit and the most fearsome happenings in the sky – lighting and thunder. His throne is a place of power.

His throne is also a place of worship, for power and godliness go together with Him. They are usually separate on earth, which is why earthly powers often oppose God's people throughout the book, but with Him, power and righteousness coincide. Therefore, He is worshipped by creatures like those of Ezekiel with words like those of Isaiah. A new and better temple is found in this throne room because His place of worship is wherever He is, not some specific place such as Jerusalem. Here, even the highest honors, such as the crowns of the elders, are cast down before Him because none is worthy in His sight, and all worth and worship are His alone. If we forget that, we forget everything, so all that "will take place," all things to come, proceed from this reality:

"for You created all things"[1] and therefore all power over all things and all times and all places is also Yours, O Lord.

Chapter 5

The reigning King is a Conqueror and an Interpreter. Among the elders of Israel, the Lion of Judah has conquered death and hell. That Lion is also a Lamb Who bore the whole world's sins and rose to life again after death. That Lamb is Himself, God, so that between the seated King and the sevenfold Spirit and the Lamb was slain before the foundation of the world, the Holy Trinity is worshipped in glory and working for the salvation of His people. The ransom the Lamb procured avails for people from every distinct group one could conceive of (5:9): different lines of descent, different languages, different ethnicities, different countries. From them all, the Lamb makes a single Kingdom with one King, the triune God, and a priestly people created for His worship.

Why this vision now? Is there no progress in the book's action here? Before all the actions to follow, all the strife, the prayers, and the conquest described, the source of that action and the goal of that action are the reality of God's reign and the necessity of God's worship. We understand nothing else without knowing His reign – the facts of what the Lamb's blood and resurrected life have done. Without knowing that the highest and holiest of His creatures – these strange angelic beings full of eyes as the Lamb Himself here is (5:6) – we understand nothing of what matters and what creation owes its Creator. From the mountain peak of this paradise vision, we see far more of the earth's strife, terror, and destiny.

Chapter 6

The Lamb alone has the authority to read the divinely appointed doom of the earth. What is sealed by His Father is unsealed only by Him. God's writing is the world's destiny. When the first seal is opened, a rider with a bow like the Parthians, Rome's greatest enemy, comes forth, a pagan making war on a pagan empire as Cyrus did on Babylon. The red rider brings warfare on earth, and the black rider brings famine. These deprivations of peace and food lead to the fourth rider, Death, riding on a blanched horse. The first four seals show God's judgment of wrath on earth at any time or place.

The fifth seal displays the martyrs who have already died for witnessing about Jesus, slain by ungodly earthly powers. They cry out for vengeance, and the Lord's only delay is that the appointed number of "their fellow servants and brothers" (6:11) must be complete before He will avenge their blood. This puts even martyrdom under the Lord's control, as were the works of the previous seals. What appears chaotic, violent, and terrifying to mankind is within God's control and provision, and He will bring it to pass and bring it to an end.

The sixth seal is the seal of Doomsday, the end of all things, with signs such as the radical change in heavenly bodies and earthquakes and the destruction of mountains. The

---

[1] FC SD I·34 uses 4·11 among other proofs that God created human nature and that it remains a "creature and work of God" even after the fall into sin.

terror of men at the End of all things fulfills the words of Jesus and of all the prophets concerning the wrath of God upon sin on the Last Day and the terror of men who come to the Last Day without the blood of Jesus. Lamb's cleansing blood is no longer available, and His wrath (6:16) comes swiftly for unreconciled rebels.

CHAPTER 7

Here is a harvest vision, all God's own safely gathered in. The mark on their foreheads will oppose the beast's mark to be mentioned later. Like the color of the horses in the previous chapter, their number is symbolic, the perfect number for God's people. Each tribe of Israel has the complete number of the sons of Israel (12) multiplied by a perfect number (1,000), so the complete number of 6:11 is symbolically 144,000. That does not limit God's salvation to 144,000 distinct human beings from all over the earth throughout history. It means He will complete the good work He has begun in anyone who believes and is baptized (Mk. 16:16). All His sheep will be gathered into His fold at last.

To such lambs of Christ, great promises and comfort belong. Their common song of salvation, though sung perhaps in different tongues, proclaims His everyday wonders, and they have the priestly privilege of appearing before God. The blessed join in angelic things: worship of God and rejoicing song to Him. They have a standard white garment and a common origin in the world's great tribulation. This tribulation was described in ch. 6 and not located at any one specific time. Tribulation was the state of mankind upon the earth before the world's end, and the blessed passed through tribulation to find the rest and joys of Paradise before God and before His Lamb. That rest obtains the freedoms Christ promises in the Beatitudes, the vision long sought and hoped for, and they are released even from tears because God finally wipes away the teardrops from His children's eyes. Even what was not sinful since Jesus Himself wept (Jn. 10:35) but resulted from the sadness of sin and death is done away with. Their lives are wholly transformed and yet theirs. They have not become angels in heaven. They have become men without sin and at rest in God, as they were always meant to be.

> *A book symbolically written must be symbolically read. Thunder, rumblings, flashes of lightning, and an earthquake need not be specific weather systems or slippages in tectonic plates. They are signs of imminent destruction visited throughout history in particular places such as Sodom, Egypt, or Jerusalem that point toward and accompany the final destruction of wickedness and an earth full of violence and wickedness. All those signs have now reached their destination, and the end of the road entirely comes in the destruction of the old world before bringing a new heavens and a new earth in which righteousness dwells. We put all Scripture's signs together to find what Scripture prophesies, not dividing the signs from one another or looking for them in their fullness before the world's complete end.*

Chapter 8

From this point, God's thunder rolls for four chapters, from this salvation of the blessed down to the final destruction of the wicked at the end of chapter 11. The seven seals opened will lead to seven trumpets blown (8:6-11:15), so that the destruction of the wicked will match the salvation of the blessed, as one finds everywhere in Scripture. Salvation and judgment occur at the same time. The Day of the Lord is a terror to His foes and a joy to His people.

The old world's destruction proceeds from Heaven's throne. The censer full of the prayers of the blessed is the angelic source of the world's fiery end. What was begun out of water and once deluged by water is ended by fire. With that fire are many other signs of the end, as the prophets foretold.

The angels' trumpets – instruments for war and judgment throughout Scripture – announce the end of earth's growth (6:7), the sea (6:9), fresh water (6:11), and the heavenly bodies (6:12), with more woes to come. The creation is coming undone, as Job had hoped for himself in his misery, and as men are terrified to see in their unreadiness for God's wrath to be completed.

Chapter 9

The work of Satan, the "star fallen from heaven to earth," is pictured as of short duration. The world is coming undone while Satan is still abroad on the earth. His time is short because the world's time is short. That puts the "end times" already in our times when Satan is now at work but can harm only those who are not sealed by Christ (9:4). Christ's people need not fear this fallen light-bearer (the meaning of "Lucifer"). His work and the work of his monstrous destroyers (see 9:7-11) is the work of destruction. God controls such work and releases such destruction, which is only one woe among others. Satan is no competitor to God but subject to His decree. The King has no rival.

Even the destruction wrought by the sixth woe and the angels riding horses with the heads of lions (9:17) does not convince mankind to change its ways. What is pictured here is the desperate nature of the end times. God's judgments are unfolded, and the time is lengthened to give men time for repentance, but for all the warnings and all the mercies, men do not turn from their evil and live (9:20). They remain in their filth and love to have it so (9:20-21).

Chapter 10

Like all sevens in the book, the seventh angel brings to completion these destructions and these woes. This final, seventh destruction and final, third woe will be carried out through John's prophesying because what is written is first eaten. John is a prophet like Ezekiel, consuming God's Word and then delivering that Word to the nations.[2] As salvation is available to all nations, destruction is brought upon all nations, too, none

---

[2] SA III.III.30 uses 10-11 to describe John as the "fiery angel...the true preacher of repentance" who hurls those buying and selling works into one heap when he commands repentance.

excepted, neither Jew nor Gentile. What was available to all is, therefore, the grounds of accountability for all because all the earth must worship Him alone, and John shall be the messenger of that salvation. John's vivid pictures are always united with this straightforward message constantly repeated in the book: Repent and live!

Chapter 11

The measurement of God's house is a prophetic sign of the Lord's excelling mercies and promises fulfilled. What was delayed – being in God's presence, being at rest, serving Him as priests do – is now at hand, and the prophet or here the apostle is as delighted to measure the temple, the place of God's dwelling with His people, as Moses was to recount the geography of Eden. Here is a survey that blesses. The lines have truly fallen for us "in pleasant places," from this survey, we know we have a "beautiful inheritance." The measurement has its limits because the apostle prophesies at a time when the complete End has not yet come. For now, the nations still trample Jerusalem. This displays the tribulation the church still undergoes before its complete safety. During that time, God keeps for Himself witnesses on the earth, testifying to His mercies and His judgments.

Those witnesses are here two in number as were the original witnesses Jesus sent out. They are no specific individuals from the church's history, but they are two flourishing trees (Psalm 1) and two lampstands (1:20) because they are righteous men who have God's Word on their lips. Like the three young men in Babylon, they are protected, and like James the Just, they will die for their testimony (11:8) in a place full of wickedness, symbolized by Sodom's unrighteousness and Egypt's impiety. For a time halfway to completion (3 1/2 is one-half of 7), the earth will deny God's witnesses the honor they deserve, not even allowing them to be buried. The world rejoices at the death of God's servants (11:10) because God's Word is irksome to fallen man, but the resurrection of God's servants (similar to the resurrections of Lazarus and of the saints at Jesus' resurrection. If they are translated like Enoch, it is to escape the destruction (7 x 1,000 = 7,000 killed in 11:13) that God's judgment wreaks. This second woe is a woe upon the rejection of God's messengers, as the first woe was upon the unsealed, those not belonging to Christ. Each woe is a different facet of the same problem: rejecting the reign of the Lamb.

Chapter 12

Here is this book's center and heart. It lies in the middle of woes and prophecies proclaimed on either side of it, and it unfolds the central drama of the heavenly warfare pictured throughout the book. The dragon sought to kill the Holy Child, and he could not. Satan sought Christ's destruction, and yet the Lamb reigns.

Notice how 12:1-6 concerns something we do not see in the Gospels: the threat to the Virgin and to her Holy Child.[3] We imagine that her first pregnancy was difficult but not what Satan had in his heart to do. As with all else in Revelation, what's here displayed

---

3   12.1ff is the identification of the pope as the lion crying out against God's truth and commanding obedience to himself as the antichrist in SA II.IV.4.

is the warfare of God and Satan that mortals do not see, but that determines our eternal destiny. These unseen things are the sum and substance of whether we perish eternally or live eternally. The destruction of Satan (12:9) is the end of our woes and our peril. The victory of God and His Christ (12:10) ends our accusation, the law's "sting."

The woman's flight in the wilderness pictures both Mary's danger and the church's, for all who adhere to Jesus are pictured here as her children, as the church is our mother, a Jerusalem above the earthly city. As Christ was born of Mary, Christians are born of the church, and Satan's threats during his short time were first toward Mary and then toward the church. If he cannot assault Christ and has already been conquered in heaven, he will make his attempt on the Christians who dwell here on earth, but we will be nourished in a desert place like Elijah fleeing from Jezebel and be kept safe, even if the ravens must feed us. We will endure. The church shall remain. We will conquer.

Chapter 13

The two beasts are demonic counterparts to the two heavenly witnesses of Ch. 11. Satan is not creative and can only mimic and pervert what God creates. The beasts, as does the Lamb, have many eyes and wear a crown as He does. They are adorned with blasphemies as He is adorned with holiness. They have many names, as pagans always do, and He has only one Name that God gives. They pretend to have His power. They desire the worship only He deserves. They are His inversion, and their destiny is thus death, not the life He has.

The first beast has many powers and receives worship from "the whole earth" (13:3), a unity in ungodliness bringing the entire world together. He also has his wonders; though he was wounded for a time, he is healed. The presence of wonders is not evidence of God's presence, for Satan has his miracles and messengers, as does the Lord. The difference is in the message: the beast utters blasphemies for a time of incompletion (7 x 6 = 42 months). He cannot blaspheme forever, but all who are not God's, whose names are not written in the Lamb's book of life (13:8), shall worship this blasphemer. The words of Jesus about having ears to hear are always needed when differences among men are revealed: the fruitful seed distinct from the unfruitful seed fallen among thorns, the saints distinct from worshippers of the beast. We expect the beast to arise and should not be startled when many follow so that we can endure and trust in Christ (13:10).

So, the famous mark of the beast (13:18) is no memorable name or number, as some suggest it symbolizes the emperor Nero's name, a suggestion that only works in Aramaic, not in Greek, the book's language. The mark is known through its action: you cannot live on this earth with its beastly rulers without this mark. It is a mark of ownership, an inversion of God's sealing of His saints on their foreheads because the beasts dress up as God. The second beast serves the first beast as the sword serves the prophet, making the earth worship the first beast through force (13:12). So, its sign or mark is whatever anywhere denotes allegiance to blasphemy. That mark could be all sorts of things at many times and places: a crescent over a mosque or a rainbow flag outside a business today.

The significance is always the same: earthly power is everything, this world will never end, God is not King, so bow down! The saints need endurance and faith in Christ because the world may oppose them as the world's prince, Satan, opposed the Holy Child, but He conquers, and we, too, finally conquer.

CHAPTER 14

Dwelling with the Lamb are His holy ones. Their holiness is not in abstention from marriage, but like all the book's other symbols, they have kept themselves from Jezebel and the self-destruction of sexual immorality. The three angels announce the gospel, the doom of evil, and the destiny of idolaters. All those are for "the endurance of the saints" (14:12) who are prone to forget the gospel, neglect the reality of evil, and fall into idolatry (cf. Ps. 1). The reaping and the harvest winepress show a picture of the absolute end of this old earth, one picture among many because the Apocalypse shows the same realities from a variety of successive angles rather than following a single timeline through the whole book.

CHAPTER 15

God's wrath proceeds from His sanctuary. He is not separate from His wrath, but men must remain separated from Him – not even to enter the sanctuary (15:8) – until that wrath is in the past with the unleashing of seven plagues. The carrying out of His wrath and the announcement of His salvation are angels' work, who do whatever He commands. The blessed who sing are not themselves angels but rather conquerors over this world's evils (15:2) through the Lamb, and their destiny, even before the world's end, is the praise of the world's Maker. Their praise of His justice (15:3) is praise of the wrath He sends on an unjust earth. The saints do not find His justice to be fearsome but righteous, not embarrassing to admit but worthy of high song.

CHAPTER 16

Since we have seen the world end before and God's wrath poured out before, the general outline of this chapter is unsurprising: God is just in His judgments. The particulars of the three sets of seven lie like the instruments of judgment. Seven seals stand for seven things only the Lamb can unlock and show. Seven trumpets stand for seven warlike blasts against evil and announcements of its doom. Seven bowls are seven measures of judgment that must be measured out on an earth full of violence and wickedness.

The judgments on the unbelieving Pharaoh and his kingdom Egypt are here worked out on the entire unbelieving world and its symbolic ruler, the beast. Creation itself is dried up and destroyed, and the desperate beast gathers his forces for a final war on righteousness at Armageddon. The outpourings and the warfare precede the final bowl (16:17), which is accompanied by the signs of divine judgment and control over the creation (16:18), indicating the destruction of Babylon as the center of evil and all in league with that wicked city, also called Sodom and Egypt. This Babylon may be Rome (as in 1 Peter), but it also always stands for the concentration of evil in one place, a place of might and arrogance, from Babel to Nineveh to our modern cities.

Chapter 17

At the pinnacle of might and arrogance is the woman whom the blessed do not know. She personifies the immorality and murder that evil loves to foster. Unlike the woman of Ch. 12, unlike the Mother of God and Mother Church, she gives birth to nothing but deceives men into loving her. She is fruitless and lures to vanity, and she is nourished not miraculously as the woman in the wilderness. Still, on the shed blood of God's saints (17:6). She is a mother only of prostitutes and abominations, not of children (17:5).

The array of kings allied to the beast will destroy that woman in her pride. Like Cyrus conquering Babylon, the beast with his worshippers will conquer this Babylonian prostitute. In this way, God makes war on His enemies through having His enemies make war on one another. When they raise their hands against Him to dethrone Him, He will conquer with His faithful saints (17:14). The dissension of the evil from one another is a great comfort to the saints who know that they are allied with their King while the wicked are at war not only with their King but also with one another until destruction finds all the wicked at the end.

Chapter 18

Overturned and emptied, Babylon becomes like a bowl tipped over and wiped clean. Like the cities subject to God's judgment throughout the Old Testament from Nineveh to Jerusalem, Babylon sings her pride (18:4-8) before others sing her death song (18:10, 14, 16-17, 19-20, 21-24). Now when the mighty of the earth (18:9) and the wealthy of the world (18:11, 15) and those who roam throughout the earth as if they were both mighty and wealthy (18:17, to which compare the seafarers of Jonah and of James) are all dismayed, there is song, which is fitting for high and amazing times. No pedestrian description of lowered living standards or high vacancy rates for homes and apartments would do what poetry here does. The angel casts a millstone into the sea as a judgment on the perversion of Babylon. The millstone hung around the neck was sure to drown the one who made the little ones stumble. Like "a great millstone" cast into the sea, the stone will end Babylon's commerce forever. All the deceit in its finery has ended.

Chapter 19

This is the glorious companion to the judgments of the previous chapter: likewise full of song and of the final destiny of a Leader Who here is as good as the prostitute was wicked, as full of righteousness as she was unrighteousness, and like her, He shares His destiny with His servants. The servants of the prostitute and the beast are consigned to an eternal fire even as they are food for scavenging birds, the end of all deserted cities, and their denizens. The servants of the Lamb worship Him in glory and come to the marriage supper. It is a rare element of the synoptic gospels in the Apocalypse, where the marriage supper is the end of all things and the blessed feast there. The wicked are feasted upon, and the victorious King rides out in conquest to conquer.

CHAPTER 20

The millennial reign, Satan's downfall, and judgment are all signs and symbols of the End of all things. If they were intended to be a literal one-thousand-year timespan, a specific battle at some point in history, or a separate event of judgment distinct from all the others in the book, they would not be placed inside a vision full of symbols. Instead, they are rich symbols with much to help the saints patiently endure the present time and its sufferings.

The one thousand years are this present age when the saints give testimony to Christ and resist the beast's mark (20:4). After this time, all the dead shall rise (20:5), and then comes the judgment. The first resurrection one finds through faith ensures a second resurrection on the Last Day and protection from the "second death" (20:6). The warfare that Satan now makes with all his forces is symbolized in "Gog and Magog" (20:8). Still, the destiny of all the wicked is the "lake of fire and sulfur" (20:10). The final judgment God renders will be based on two books. One is a book of men's deeds (20: 12), and of that one book, there are many volumes or "books" (20:12). There is only one "book of life" (20:12) in which the Lamb writes men's names, and if their names are found there in the book of life, they live. If their names are found solely in the book of their deeds, they die. Only the Lamb, not men's deeds, protects from the second death of the judgment.

CHAPTERS 21-22

The jewels, the angels, the numeric perfection, the presence of all the sons of Jacob, and the name of the holy city all signify that here again, God is dwelling with man as in the Garden at the beginning. Our end is our beginning, yet the end is better than the beginning. In the beginning, the heavenly bodies gave light and marked time. In the end, the Lamb is Himself our Light. In the beginning, there was a possibility of evil's intrusion. In the end, all evil is excluded (21:8). In the end, pain, crying, and death are no more, and Woman is perfected as the Church, the Bride of the Lamb (20:9).

The river pours forth in all seasons, and there is always fruit, a perpetual fruitfulness so different from the fruitlessness of wickedness. Having held forth this vision to His servants, the Lamb encourages them to hold fast to His words in this present time before the fulfillment of this vision. Forward they strive and do not neglect His words. The realities of that time of blessing, the Spirit, and the perfected Bride of the Lamb admonish the saint now suffering to come and find the peace and true drink he needs. Jesus sets His seal on the book (22:20) and promises that He is coming again soon to a dying world that those who hear and believe His book should live forever.

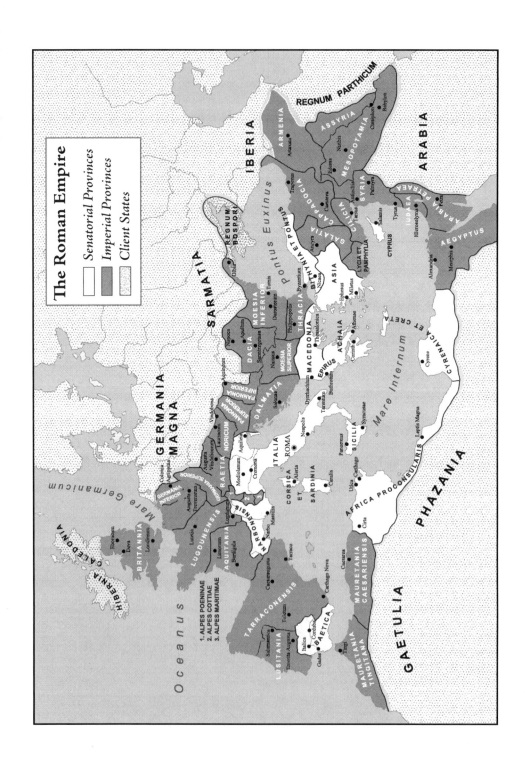

About the AUTHOR

Adam C. Koontz is the pastor of Redeemer Lutheran Church and School, Oakmont, Pennsylvania. He and his wife, Jen, have nine children and make their home in Plum, Pennsylvania.

Forthcoming by the AUTHOR

THE FAMILY BIBLE COMMENTARY

Old Testament: The Book of Genesis - The Book of Deuteronomy (Volume I, December 2025).

Old Testament: The Book of Joshua - The Book of Esther (Volume II, December 2026).

Old Testament: The Book of Job - The Book of Malachi (Volume III, December 2027).

INDEX

A

Abraham, 21–22, 27, 49–52, 86–88, 98

Adam, 23, 35, 52, 109, 113

adiaphoron, 35

afflictions, 43, 58, 102, 105, 111

allegory, 49, 51

angelic powers, 61–62

angels, 37–38, 51, 61–62, 64, 66, 69, 83–84, 89, 103, 108, 120–122, 128, 133–134, 137, 139

anger, 71, 95

antichrist, 64, 68–69, 112–113, 116–117, 135

apostasy, 68–69, 86

arrogance, 119, 138

atonement, 22, 90

authority, 37, 46, 49, 57, 62, 68, 71, 74, 80, 82, 106, 121, 132

B

Babylon, 101, 106, 132, 135, 137–138

baptism, 23–24, 33, 39, 62–63, 80, 105–106, 114

beasts, 70, 136

bishops, 68, 72, 99, 104–106, 108

blasphemy, 62, 88, 108, 136

blood, 22–25, 28, 33, 36–38, 46, 52, 55, 59, 62, 84, 87–90, 102–103, 106, 111, 114, 132–133, 138

body of Christ, 27, 37–38, 45, 107

book of life, 25, 130, 136, 139

brothers, 28, 33–34, 49–50, 52, 66–67, 78, 90, 100, 106, 112–113, 115, 119, 132

false, 13, 36, 46–47, 49–50, 52, 58, 61–63, 69, 77–79, 99, 107–108, 112–116, 118, 120–122, 129–130

weak, 28–29, 35–36, 47, 55, 68, 87, 102, 129, 131

C

Cain, 67, 71, 89, 121

callings, 35, 56, 63, 76

captivity, 53–54, 57–58, 61, 70, 75, 78, 81

care, 40, 54, 57, 65, 73, 81, 116

childbearing, 71

children, 13, 25–26, 37, 41, 44–45, 47, 51, 55–57, 59, 65, 69, 71, 110, 112–113, 115–116, 119, 130, 133, 136, 138

Christ, 13–14, 19–47, 49–69, 71–90, 97–98, 100–116, 118–119, 122, 127–131, 133–137, 139

Christ Jesus, 13, 22, 43, 49, 60, 68, 73, 77, 81, 84, 100, 113, 127

Christ's blood, 22, 24–25, 36, 84, 88, 103, 114

Christ's Body, 36–37, 39, 52, 62, 111

Christ's Church, 26, 68

Christ's covenant, 87–88

Christ's judgment, 66, 76

Christ's resurrection, 39, 103, 109

Christ's sacrifice, 44, 87–88

Christ's teachings, 103

Christ's truth, 68, 112, 119

Christ's way, 25, 35–36, 40, 56, 59

Christ's Word, 60, 63

Christ's work, 44, 83, 111

Christian churches, 72, 115

Christian life, 33, 102, 110, 129

Christian Ministry, 42

Christian worship, 62, 89

Christianity, 36, 59–60, 104, 111, 119, 130–131

Christians, 20, 23, 25, 28–29, 33–37, 40–41, 45, 47, 49–53, 56–57, 60, 63–66, 68–69, 74–75, 78, 83, 95, 98, 101–107, 110, 112–113, 116–119, 129–130, 136

Church, 13–14, 23, 25–27, 29–34, 36–38, 40–42, 44–75, 77–79, 82, 85, 89–90, 95, 97–103, 105–106, 108, 110, 112, 115–117, 119–121, 127–131, 135–136, 138–139

circumcision, 21, 48–49, 52, 55, 59, 89

cleansing, 88, 111, 114, 133

collection, 28, 30, 40–42, 45, 48

communion, 33, 36–37, 40, 107, 110, 121

consciences, 23, 44, 63

  good, 13, 21–29, 33, 35–36, 38–39, 44, 53, 57–60, 66, 69, 71–74, 76, 78–80, 82, 86–87, 97–99, 101, 104–108, 116, 119, 130–131, 133, 138

conversion, 20, 26, 54, 65, 71

D

damnation, 24, 68, 108

dangers, 36, 50, 96, 99, 106–108, 110, 116, 121

Daniel, 64, 89, 128–129

David, 22, 27

deacons, 72

deceit, 24, 63, 103–104, 138

deception, 62, 66, 69, 97, 111, 113, 116–117, 119–121

delights, 13, 120

demons, 36, 51, 62, 68, 73, 77, 108, 130

destruction, 28, 50, 56, 60, 66–67, 99, 108–109, 121–122, 127, 132–138

devil, 20, 44, 97, 109, 122

discernment, 37, 66, 86

disciples, 13, 32, 75, 77, 103, 111–112, 118, 130

discipline, 33, 35, 70, 89, 96

divine judgment, 32, 67, 137

divine nature, 83, 85, 97, 107–108

Divine Service, 87–89, 98

divorce, 34, 73, 86

Doomsday, 132

E

Egypt, 24, 133, 135, 137

elders, 72, 74, 99, 104–106, 116, 131–132

election, 19, 25–27, 108, 111

emotions, 31, 56

encouragement, 28, 75, 90, 96, 102

errors, 47, 62, 71, 78, 118

ethnicities, 63, 132

Ezekiel, 41, 127–129, 131, 134

F

faith, 19–23, 26–27, 29, 38, 42, 47, 49–55, 57, 65–66, 68, 70–72, 76–77, 83, 86, 88–89, 95–100, 102–103, 106–115, 117, 120, 137, 139

dead, 23–25, 27, 31, 39, 42–43, 55, 58, 90, 96, 98, 111, 139
false teaching, 50, 61–63, 99, 107, 113, 115, 120
falsehood, 46, 61–62, 71, 73, 77, 79, 109, 115, 118, 121
fear of God, 31, 74
fellowship, 40, 110–112, 119, 130
food, 35–36, 50, 62, 73–74, 86, 129, 132, 138
forgiveness, 22, 33, 42, 44, 87, 89, 112, 114–115
freedom, 23–25, 28, 35, 43, 49–50, 52, 61, 80, 82, 121, 133
fruit, 24, 27, 52, 58, 63, 66, 69, 72, 79–80, 83, 86, 97, 99, 107, 139
fruitless, 13, 53, 58, 71, 77, 83, 86, 121, 138
fulfillment, 83, 87, 109, 139

G

genealogy, 21, 27, 71, 105
Gentile Christians, 40, 50
gentleness, 52, 69, 77
gifts, 25, 27, 30, 32, 37–40, 45, 54, 56, 58–59, 70, 73, 84, 95–97, 99, 105, 113
God, 13–14, 19–39, 41–60, 62–63, 65–68, 70–74, 76–77, 79–80, 82–90, 95–116, 119–121, 127–139
gospel, 19–20, 22, 25–27, 29, 35, 39–40, 42–52, 54–55, 58–59, 64–70, 74, 76, 78–79, 81–85, 96–97, 101, 104, 108–111, 115, 118–120, 128–129, 135, 137–138
government, 23, 28, 72, 104
grace, 13, 19, 22, 24–27, 31, 47, 55, 63, 71, 80, 84, 88, 102, 106, 109, 114
   election of, 19, 25, 27
guilt, 21

H

harvest, 45, 58, 86, 99, 133, 137
hearts, 13, 21, 26, 42, 67, 74, 82, 85, 88, 103, 114–115
hell, 14, 25, 68, 105, 132
holiness, 33, 41, 44, 50, 73, 88, 102, 136–137
Holy Trinity, 59, 102, 132
home, 25, 36, 44, 63, 73, 79, 82, 89, 102, 113–114, 118, 138
honor, 27, 43, 66, 77, 84–85, 87, 131, 135
hostility, 46, 55, 65
household, 37, 50, 54–55, 61, 63, 79, 104, 116
humiliation, 59
husbands, 57, 104
hypocrisy, 27, 50, 74

I

idolatry, 33, 36, 50, 56, 62, 65, 103, 114–115, 130, 137
idols, 13, 28, 34–36, 85, 114–115
images, 107, 114, 120, 128, 131
imitate, 36, 38, 40, 50, 66, 71, 86, 119
imitation, 66, 69, 77
immorality, 130, 137–138
inheritance, 49, 102, 105, 108, 135
instruments, 38, 134, 137
intercession, 58, 61, 71
Isaac, 26, 51–52, 88
Isaiah, 23, 30–31, 41, 61, 67, 101, 131
Israel, 14, 19, 24, 26–27, 29, 36, 43, 45, 50, 54, 88, 90, 97, 105, 130–133

J

Jacob, 75, 88, 139

Jesus, 13, 22–23, 25, 27, 29, 31–32, 34–36, 38–40, 42–43, 47, 49, 51, 57, 60, 63, 65–66, 68, 73, 77, 81, 83–89, 95–100, 104, 109–110, 112–113, 115–116, 118–120, 127–128, 132–133, 135–136, 139

Jesus' blood, 22

Jesus' death, 86

Jesus' resurrection, 31, 135

Jesus' teaching, 99

Jewish myths, 79

Jews, 21–22, 25–27, 29, 35–36, 40, 49–50, 55–56, 65, 83, 88, 90, 101, 105, 129, 131

Jezebel, 130, 136–137

Joseph, 88, 120

Joshua, 83, 85, 98

joy, 24, 32, 41, 57–58, 60, 62, 103, 113, 119, 129, 133–134

Judaism, 49, 69, 83

Judas, 50, 67

Judea, 40, 42, 65, 118

judgment, 21, 32–33, 37–39, 44, 64, 66–67, 74, 76, 84, 96, 98, 100, 105, 109, 111, 122, 128, 130, 132, 134–135, 137–139

Judgment Day, 76, 105

justice, 22, 28, 68, 109, 137

justification, 20–23, 33, 37, 49–50, 52–53, 55, 98, 102

K

kindness, 77, 80, 102, 116

King, 23–24, 43, 46–47, 68, 71, 87, 127–128, 130–132, 134, 137–139

kingdom, 14, 23–24, 28, 39, 42, 67, 73, 79, 84, 89, 104, 130, 132, 137

knowledge, 21, 28, 33, 37, 42, 46, 51, 54, 58, 62, 67, 71, 73, 77, 85–86, 101, 104, 109, 112–113, 128–129

L

Lamb, 40, 102, 110, 128, 132–133, 135–139

Lamb of God, 128

languages, 37, 39, 132

Last Day, 23, 25, 33, 37–38, 40, 60, 62, 64–65, 74–75, 103, 133, 139

law, 19–22, 24–27, 31, 35–36, 38, 42–43, 46–53, 55, 59, 63, 69–71, 81–85, 87–90, 95–98, 103, 111, 136

law of Christ, 35–36, 81

lawless, 71, 80

lawlessness, 67–68, 80

man of, 44, 67–68, 97, 118

letters, 13–14, 24, 29–30, 32, 42, 57–58, 61, 65, 68, 75, 82, 84, 101, 107–110, 112, 115–116, 118–119, 121, 127–128, 131

Levi, 87

liars, 73

life, 13–14, 19–28, 31–40, 42–44, 46, 48–66, 69–77, 79–80, 82–89, 98–106, 108–114, 116, 121–122, 127, 129–130, 132–133, 136, 139

church's, 13, 25, 27, 30, 33, 37, 44, 46–47, 57, 72–74, 77, 79, 89–90, 102, 105–106, 116, 127–129, 135–136

eternal, 20, 28, 38, 40, 53, 57, 59, 62, 67–68, 76, 80, 84, 86–87, 89, 102, 104, 108–109, 114, 122, 127, 136, 138

light, 13–14, 31, 44, 54, 56, 59–60, 76, 87, 103, 108, 111, 128, 134, 139

lips, 62, 135

Lord's Day, 40, 45

Lord's Supper, 36–37, 47

love, 20, 22–23, 25, 27–31, 33–34, 38–40, 44, 46–47, 52, 55–57, 62–67, 69, 71–72, 74, 76–82, 84, 89, 96–100, 103, 105, 107–116, 119, 121–122, 127, 129, 131, 134, 138

lovelessness, 38–39, 110

lust, 63, 108

M

male headship, 23

mark, 21, 35, 38, 44, 66, 82, 95, 101, 133, 136, 139

marriage, 30, 34, 36, 39, 56, 66, 71, 73, 90, 104, 137–138

marriage and childbearing, 71

marriage bed, 34

martyrdom, 53, 115, 132

Mary, 97, 136

mediator, 49, 71, 87, 111

Melchizedek, 83, 85–87

members, 24, 26, 30, 44, 52, 63, 73, 77, 95, 99, 101, 112, 115

merit, 31, 53, 55, 63, 103, 107

ministers, 13, 32, 45, 52, 58, 66, 70–72, 74–77, 99, 105, 116, 119–120

ministers of Christ, 32, 119

ministry, 20, 25, 27, 29, 38, 40–49, 53–54, 56, 61, 64, 67, 70–77, 87, 101, 103, 105, 115, 118–119, 127

misery, 24, 100, 134

money, 28, 45, 74, 77, 106

Moses, 22, 24–25, 35, 42–43, 46–47, 49–51, 75, 81, 83–85, 87–89, 96, 121, 135

mother, 51, 65, 76, 116, 136, 138

N

nations, 21, 25–27, 29, 39, 46, 53, 55, 62, 71, 85, 103, 130–131, 134–135

nature, 20, 34, 41–43, 47, 51, 53–55, 62, 64, 67, 69, 73, 78–79, 83–86, 97, 99, 102–103, 105, 107–108, 110–111, 120, 132, 134

necessity, 65, 82, 106, 132

neighbor, 28, 65, 98, 105

new covenant, 84–85, 87

O

oath, 85, 96, 100

obedience of faith, 20, 26

old covenant, 64, 84, 87

opponents, 47, 50, 55, 60, 71, 73, 75, 78–79, 84, 88

oracles, 21, 26

oracles of God, 26

order, 22, 28, 37, 39, 56–57, 65, 70, 72, 79, 85–86, 104, 121

overseers, 72, 78

P

paradise, 131–133

partiality, 96, 98, 100

passions, 20, 52, 96, 104–106, 108, 110, 120

pastors, 32, 99, 104, 119

pattern, 23, 28, 31, 38, 59–60, 70–71, 74, 96, 107, 110, 113, 121, 127

Paul's time, 61, 68–69

peace, 23–24, 26, 33, 51, 53, 55, 60, 62, 66, 85, 95, 99, 118, 132, 139

persecution, 13, 65, 68, 83, 95, 97, 101, 103–104, 107, 118, 128–129, 131

person of Christ, 105, 111

personal union, 62, 84, 103

power, 13, 20–21, 23, 25, 27–28, 31, 42, 44, 46–47, 49, 51, 53–55, 57–58,

60–63, 67–69, 73, 76–77, 84, 86, 96, 98–100, 102–106, 110–111, 129, 131–132, 136

prayers, 29, 57, 63, 65, 71, 114, 132, 134

preachers, 13, 32, 46, 53, 58, 71, 77

preaching, 13, 19–20, 25–26, 29, 31, 38–39, 42–48, 51, 54, 65, 70–72, 74, 76–80, 101–102, 104, 111, 120

preaching office, 120

predestination, 25, 54, 109, 111

pride, 21, 44, 77, 99–100, 138

priesthood, 58, 83–84, 86–87, 103–104, 106

priests, 32, 85, 87, 103–104, 135

principles, 45, 51, 62–63

prophets, 19, 22, 43, 46, 55, 96, 101, 111, 116, 118, 121, 127, 133–134

Q

qualifications, 41, 46, 60, 72, 78–79, 96

R

rapture, 66

rejection, 60, 103, 118, 135

remission, 63, 107, 111

repentance, 37, 39, 85–86, 100, 105, 114, 134

resurrection, 13, 23, 30–31, 38–40, 44, 47, 53, 58–60, 63–64, 75–77, 86, 103, 105, 109, 127, 135, 139

return, 13, 24, 34, 42, 44, 50–51, 65–66, 68–69, 85, 90, 105, 110, 130

riches, 55, 96, 100

righteousness, 20, 22–24, 26, 51, 57–58, 63, 71, 109, 111, 128, 131, 133, 137–138

S

Sabbath, 85, 88

sacrifices, 27, 35, 41, 43–44, 83, 103

saints, 33, 40, 66, 103, 105–106, 120, 127, 135–139

salvation, 20, 22, 25–27, 29, 35–36, 41, 49–51, 53–55, 57, 59, 67–69, 73, 76, 84–86, 96, 101–102, 105, 115, 121, 132–135, 137

Satan, 28, 32–33, 42–43, 57, 68–69, 71, 74, 77, 90, 105–106, 108, 112–113, 116, 129, 134–137, 139

   works of, 31, 50, 98, 105, 113–114, 132

Savior, 21–22, 25, 29, 51, 62, 70, 72, 85, 111

self-control, 34, 76, 107, 130

servants, 32, 72, 78, 132, 135, 138–139

service, 13, 24, 29, 36, 39, 42, 45–46, 76, 80–83, 87–89, 98, 104, 108

sheep, 100, 119, 121, 133

sickness, 37, 58, 130

signs, 69–70, 129, 132–134, 137, 139

silver, 22, 53, 103, 105

sin, 19–25, 27, 31, 33–36, 40, 42–44, 47, 51–52, 56, 62–63, 68, 71–72, 74, 80, 83–89, 95, 97, 103, 105, 107–114, 132–133

sinful natures, 78

sinners, 13, 20–22, 24, 42, 44, 50, 52, 55, 71, 89, 96

slavery, 23–25, 43, 51, 80–81

Sodom, 121, 133, 135, 137

stars, 97, 128

stone, 21, 27, 42, 84, 90, 138

strength, 35, 46, 58, 69, 78, 100, 128

submission, 27, 38, 56–57, 80

subordination, 104–105

suffering, 23, 25, 41–44, 46, 50, 54–55, 58–60, 62, 65, 76–78, 84, 101–102, 104–106, 129, 139

sword, 28, 136

T

teachers, 21, 47, 58, 61–63, 77–79, 96, 99, 104, 107–108, 113, 115–116, 120–121

temple, 27, 32, 34, 36, 38, 44, 53–55, 83–84, 87–88, 90, 100, 103–104, 127, 129, 131, 135

  new, 13–14, 19–21, 24, 26, 29, 35, 37, 40–44, 51, 53, 60–64, 68–70, 76, 78–79, 81–82, 84–85, 87, 99, 101, 103–106, 109–111, 113–114, 116, 120–121, 127–131, 133

temptation, 36, 90, 96–97, 100, 102

thanksgiving, 27–28, 30, 35–36, 45, 48, 58–64, 67, 73, 75, 103

thorn in the flesh, 46

Timothy, 23, 32, 41–44, 51, 54, 57–59, 61, 64–65, 67, 70–80

Titus, 41–45, 49, 61, 70–71, 77–80

traditions, 37, 61–63, 68

trials, 23, 95–97, 100, 102, 106, 108

tribulation, 64, 66, 128–129, 131, 133, 135

truth, 21, 26–27, 34, 39, 46, 54, 57, 61–63, 65–66, 68–69, 73, 77, 79–80, 85–86, 95, 100, 103, 109–113, 115–119, 121, 129, 135

tutor, 32, 51

U

unbelief, 21, 26–27, 69, 71–72, 85

unbelievers, 33, 39, 42, 109

uncertainties, 13

uncircumcision, 55

V

vessels, 27, 77

victory, 25, 28, 35, 39, 51, 105, 112, 127, 129, 136

violence, 133, 137

visions, 46, 127–128

vocation, 51, 70–71

W

war, 24, 28, 57, 76, 99–100, 129, 132, 134, 137–138

warfare, 46, 54, 57, 78, 129, 132, 135–137, 139

weakness, 25, 35, 46–47, 55, 59

wilderness, 36, 83–85, 89–90, 121, 130, 136, 138

wisdom, 14, 27, 30–32, 37, 56, 73, 76, 79, 96, 99–100, 109, 112

woman, 20, 29, 37, 52, 56–57, 71–73, 77, 79, 104, 116, 130, 136, 138–139

worldliness, 30, 32, 34, 79

worship, 30–31, 37–39, 61–63, 68, 89, 104, 114, 128, 131–133, 135–136, 138

worship of angels, 61

wrath, 20, 22–23, 26–28, 36, 55–56, 59, 63, 84, 97, 108, 132–134, 137

Z

Zechariah, 54, 64, 127

Made in the USA
Columbia, SC
13 November 2024

ce417a3a-b600-44f5-8f69-5e1a54b89180R02